PERSONAL TITANIC MOMENTS

When Personal Sink-or-Swim Decisions Result in Life-Changing Moments

Personal Titanic Moments

When Personal Sink-or-Swim Decisions Result in Life-Changing Moments

Compiled and Edited by Yvonne Lehman

GRACE PUBLISHING

Grace Publishing House

Royalties for this book are donated to Samaritan's Purse.

PERSONAL TITANIC MOMENTS

When Personal Sink-or-Swim Decisions Result in Life-Changing Moments

ISBN-13: 978-1-60495-053-3

From Samaritan's Purse

We so appreciate your donating all royalties to Samaritan's Purse from the sale of the books *Divine Moments, Christmas Moments, Spoken Moments, Precious Precocious Moments, More Christmas Moments, Stupid Moments, Additional Christmas Moments, Loving Moments, Merry Christmas Moments, Cool-inary Moments, Moments with Billy Graham*, and now and now, *Personal Titanic Moments* to Samaritan's Purse.

What a blessing that you would think of us! Thank you for your willingness to bless others and bring glory to God through your literary talents. Grace and peace to you.

Their Mission Statement:

Samaritan's Purse is a nondenominational evangelical Christian organization providing spiritual and physical aid to hurting people around the world.

Since 1970, Samaritan's Purse has helped victims of war, poverty, natural disasters, disease, and famine with the purpose of sharing God's love through his son, Jesus Christ.

Go and do likewise
Luke 10:37

You can learn more by visiting their website at www.samaritanspurse.org.

Contents

Introduction Yvonne Lehman 9

1. *I Know About Loss* Robert Cook 10
2. *My Lifeboat* Diana Leagh Matthews 12
3. *Judy, Do You Trust Me?* Judith Victoria Hensley 20
4. *An Angel by My Side* Lola Di Giulio De Maci 24
5. *The Treasure* Robert W. Rettie 27
6. *The Belonging Hand* Sharon Frazier 30
7. *Landstuhl — We've Got an Emergency* Lt.Col. Robert B. Robeson 32
8. *Sufficient Grace* Bobbie Ann DuPree Foshee 37
9. *Looking for the Rainbow* Judith Vander Wege 40
10. *My Husband Gave Me 30 Days* Sheryl Boldt 41
11. *Unpredictable, Like Cloudbursts* Susan Boskat Murray 46
12. *A Tragic Day* Jonathan Hayashi 49
13. *If God Is for Us* Toni Armstrong Sample 52
14. *A Sinking Friendship* Ivette Ellis 54
15. *Courage and Sacrifice* Lt.Col. Robert B. Robeson 57
16. *Going Home* Diana C. Derringer 65
17. *Daddy's Girl* Margaret Peterson 67
18. *Journey into Exclusivity* Sherry Boykin 70
19. *But . . . the Titanic Sank* Alice Klies 73
20. *Anger's Threat* Bennie McDonald (as told to Nanette Thorsen-Snipes) 77
21. *Do You Want an Orange, Or . . . ?* Margaret Peterson 81
22. *Closing the Door* Norma C. Mezoe 85
23. *Not What I Had in Mind* Stacy Mink 88
24. *I Nearly Died* Nanette Thorsen-Snipes 91
25. *Still Afloat* Toni Armstrong Sample 94
26. *Free-Falling Without a Parachute* David Brannock 97

27. A Smooth-Sailing Night Rebecca Carpenter 100
28. Pray About It Phil Gladden 102
29. Pray Jesus, Me Lydia E. Harris 104
30. It Is Well Mirjam Budarz and Dr. Timo Budarz 106
31. That Dirty Ol' Thing? Alice Klies 109
32. Special Delivery Lt.Col. Robert Robeson 112
33. A Time for Everything Beverly Hill McKinney 118
34. How to Organize a 24-Hour Circle of Prayer Lydia E. Harris .. 120
35. Why Am I Here? Diana Leagh Matthews 122
36. Joyful Sadness Margaret Peterson 126
37. Once Upon a Cold Hot Water Day Sherri Stewart 129
38. Consuming Hopelessness Gayle Fraser 131
39. Why, God? Larry C. Hoover (as told to Helen Hoover) 133
40. Faith Is . . . ? Annmarie B. Tait 135
41. Walk of Faith Myrtle Thompson 138
42. Storms of Life Robert Cook 140
43. Losing to Gain Anne Edwards 142
44. What? Forgive Billy the Bully? Robin Bayne 145
45. Through the Dark Days Andrea Merrell 147
46. The Three Cs Rabbi Frank Stern 150
47. Love Transcends Grief Helen L. Hoover 154
48. Disintegrating Shoes Rebecca Carpenter 156
49. Guess Who's Calling Margaret Peterson 159
50. The Window of My Soul Brenda Miller 164
51. The Road Least Traveled Dr. Jayce O'Neal 166
52. The Waiting Room of Prayer Norma C. Mezoe 168
About the Authors 169

Introduction

Yvonne Lehman

Her admirers said not even God could bring down the widely-acclaimed, most beautiful, perfectly formed one the world had ever known.

Unexpectedly, she hit an unmovable object. Within four hours she was stunned, then aware of the danger and she trembled. She couldn't walk on water, so to speak, and defeated, she gave up, broke into halves, then sank into oblivion never again to see the light of day nor breathe the breath of life. The Wonder of the World, that some implied not even God could hurt, now lies to be gazed upon as a tragedy of rusty old bones.

You ever feel that way? Like an unmovable object looms right in front of you?

Unlike the ship *Titanic,* that lies on the bottom of the ocean never to rise again, the stories in this book are about people who encountered unexpected obstacles that can loom before us at any time. They may appear as an ice cube, or an iceberg.

Whether their stories are seemingly small or great, these authors have drawn the same conclusion. God can do anything. He can walk on water. He can take rusty old bones and give them life again. He says, "Take my hand and I'll take you from the cold disaster, lift you up, and teach you to bask in the warmth of my love."

1

I Know About Loss

Robert Cook

I know about loss . . .

I had begun a sermon series on the five most influential people in the Bible, excluding Jesus, and how they had all failed big time. My plan was to take five weeks to cover the five guys, not the hamburger dudes, but the influential men in the Bible. But my plans changed. On January 10th, 2015, my nineteen-year-old son hanged himself. I held vigil at his bedside for six days.

Take me instead

I begged and pleaded with God for a miracle. I offered my life in exchange for the life of my son. I believed with everything in me, God would come through and save the day. I mean, He's God. It didn't matter what the doctors said. They offered no hope, but I knew God could speak just one word, four little letters, and everything would change: "RISE!"

If I were God

I had a lot of time as I sat there to play the "if I were God" card. I explained to God, if I were you, this would be the perfect time to heal Robbie. All the doctors would instantly believe. The testimony of being raised from the brink of death would turn hundreds or even thousands to Christ. See, God? It makes perfect sense. Just say the word and it will be done. You will get all the glory. Yep, if I were God, that's how I would do it. But I'm not God, not even close.

My plans are not your plans.

My ways are not your ways. On January 16th as I held my son's head and through tears, memorized every line in his face, I felt the life leave his body. God was not going to do things my way.

In the valley

I spent the next five months in a valley so deep it's beyond comprehension. My heart shattered in a million pieces. I cry now as I write this. Some days I couldn't get out of bed, my body literally weighted down with unspeakable grief. My emotions consumed me. Life lost its joy and splendor. But I was not alone in that Valley. God was carrying me. He had to because I did not have the strength to walk. In that valley, I felt God's presence and He became more real to me than I had ever known Him to be before.

On a journey

He took me on a journey, and I experienced things I never wanted to imagine. He was molding me. Creating in me a heart that could sympathize with other parents who had or would lose a child. Months later I attended the Colorado Christian Writer's Conference as a keynote speaker.

This conference is held in a beautiful valley surrounded by majestic, snow-capped mountains.

In the five days I was there, I must have taken at least a hundred pictures of the same mountain. I was in awe of how they towered over me. I saw the handiwork of a mighty God all around me.

As I sat on the deck, drinking in the scenery, I spotted a plane flying at least 30,000 feet above me, high above the mountain range.

Perspective

I remembered when I'd flown over the same mountains two years before. The mountains looked flat from that height. There was nothing awe-inspiring about them. As the plane disappeared, I felt sorry for the people onboard. They were missing the magnificence of God I was a witness to.

In that moment, God spoke to me, "This is why I brought you through the valley." That's all He said, but all I needed to hear.

I understood perfectly.

2

My Lifeboat

Diana Leagh Matthews

I stood staring up at the large kirk (church) in Edinburg, Scotland. The sun bounced off the beautiful glass windows installed in the ancient structure, which was built around the same time the Mayflower landed on Plymouth Rock.

Taking a deep breath, I pulled open the large black doors and was overwhelmed by the enormous cathedral that surrounded me. The organ pipes loomed above the choir loft and I could not wait to hear the beautiful melodies that would emanate from this gorgeous instrument.

"May I help you?" A man stepped forward in greeting and I felt welcome.

"I'm here for the church service," I explained. Getting away from my traveling companions had not been easy. However, I had been determined to attend this church service. My soul needed time with the Lord in ways I was unable to find words to express.

"I'm sorry, but we're not having the early service today. You are welcome to stay for our service at 11:00 A.M." His Scottish brogue was thick.

I checked my watch. I'd promised my husband and his family that I would meet them at 11:00 A.M. If I were late, they would make life impossible. Not that this was anything new. Life had become difficult and unbearable on this trip, which was why I felt the need to get away and attend the kirk services that morning.

"Thank you, but I have to meet my party." I wondered if the man could see the tears forming in my eyes. I was overwhelmed, exhausted and my heart was being ripped in two.

The man studied me for a moment, when a woman walked over and greeted me. She had been standing off to the side and apparently listening to our conversation.

"We have a prayer area over there." The woman pointed towards a small alcove, which had a cross standing at the front of the area. She wrapped an arm around my shoulders and I was comforted by the gesture.

"It's okay," she whispered.

I attempted to smile through the pain filling my heart.

"Thank you." I entered the small alcove and found a bench. My mind was swimming with confusion and pain.

I walked over to the cross and noticed various papers pinned to it. Others had stood in this area with hurting hearts and written down their prayers. I picked up a piece of paper and began to write.

Forgive me for not listening to you, Lord.

Over three years ago I should have listened to the voice of God. I still remembered that day and the way my insides felt as if they were being ripped apart. In hindsight, I realized God was trying to warn me not to become involved with the man to whom I was now married. Yet I had been so in love that I told God, "I can't live without him."

Forgive me for not letting go, Lord.

For the last three years, I had been crying out to God, wondering if he had forsaken me. With each passing day, the abuse had grown greater. From the moment I moved in, I knew I had made a colossal mistake. But I had no idea how to get out of that situation. No matter how many opportunities came, I could not seem to let go of this man that had such a hold on me.

Forgive me for being so selfish, Lord.

I wasn't sure how I'd been selfish, but my husband constantly told me I was selfish and only thought about myself. Even the evening when he'd tried to force me into an intimate relationship with an extended family member, he was still telling me I was being selfish, and if I really loved him I would follow through with that despicable act.

Forgive me for hurting others, Lord.

When I moved in with this man, he had destroyed my telephone and email addresses, cutting off all contact with my family.

Forgive me for not believing you, Lord.

There were so many things my husband told me about himself, his life and his family that I no longer believed. With the passage of time and lack of evidence, the things he told me seemed to feel more like lies than truth.

Forgive me for not cherishing life, Lord.

For the three years, I'd been in this relationship all I wanted to do was die. Life did not seem worth living. On more than one occasion I tried to take my own life. The pain was so great I just wanted it to end.

After I pinned the note to the cross, I walked over to the small altar and lit a candle. There I knelt at the covered bench and bowed my head. I poured my heart out to the Father, telling him how wrong I had been and how I wished I had listened to his warnings all those years ago.

Then, I did something I had been both unable and unwilling to do for the last three years. "Father, I can't keep living this way. I believe marriage is meant to be forever, but I can't stand this roller coaster." I literally grew ill from all the ups and downs of the abuse I suffered.

"If this is where you want me, then I pray you will please reveal that to me. However, I surrender my relationship with Duncan (name changed) to you. I know there is so much more to life and I can't continue this way. Please Lord, deliver me from this situation if that is your will."

For the next two hours, I stayed in front of that altar pouring my despair out to the Lord. Although I'd accepted Christ into my heart at the age of five and had strived to live a Christian life, this was the moment I truly dedicated my all to Jesus Christ. I surrendered every part of my life, most of which I had been holding back from him, wholeheartedly over to my Savior.

I rose from where I had been kneeling with tears streaming

down my face and a heart that was much lighter. I did not hear an audible voice this day, the way I had three years ago as I walked out of my apartment for the last time. On that day when I prepared to move in with my husband, I heard the voice of God tell me, "You will lose everything before you gain the world." I had no idea at that time what God meant, but by this point I had lost everything. I had lost my freedom, my finances, all of my belongings, my hope, my peace, my career, my family and everything else I could think of.

The only thing I had not lost was my faith, but that was not due to Duncan's lack of trying. I had lost count of how many times he said, "God will not love you until you're better." At first I believed him, but when he attempted to prevent me from reading an online devotion one day and said those words, I saw him for the deceiver he truly was. I thanked God for giving me Christian parents who taught me about God's love so I could see and know this truth.

The abuse had been building for years and came to a head that August while we were in Scotland. We were away from everything that was familiar and with no way for me to seek help, the abuse broke all that I morally held dear and became my breaking point.

This was the breaking point that brought me to this moment and this Scottish church where I resubmitted and turned my life back over to God. While I heard no audible voice, I knew God heard me and was there with me.

When I met back up with my husband and his family I noticed the way he studied me for a moment. I wondered if he detected anything that was different. He did not stop with the mind games or the emotional turmoil, but the call for that detestable act no longer returned.

We returned to our Tennessee home and for the next two months I waited and prayed. Each day my prayer became more and more fervent as I screamed out for God to please help me.

Then one fall day, I once again reached my breaking point. I was so tired of hearing about all of Duncan's supposed affairs. I was really to the point I no longer cared.

After listening to the taunts for two hours that morning, I stormed out of the house and walked the twelve miles to work. I don't know how I physically walked that distance other than sheer determination.

"I can't do this any longer, Lord. Please help me. Please send me a sign if this is the person you want me to spend the remainder of my life with."

I found a place where I could gain online access, where I instantly turned to an online devotion. The scripture on the page that day was seared on my heart. *It is better to live in a corner of the housetop than in a house shared with a quarrelsome wife* (Proverbs 25:24 ESV).

Well, I had a quarrelsome husband and a quarrelsome sister-in-law, so that counted. I held those promises to my heart. Taking a deep breath, I opened my email and began to type. "I will not be returning home."

I wasn't sure what I would do or where I would go, but enough was enough.

"Help me know if I'm doing the right thing," I prayed.

When I arrived at work I was surprised to discover I could stay in some rooms nearby until I could get a paycheck or two and support myself.

"Your mother called," a co-worker said, one day. I looked at him as if he had grown horns. I had not spoken with my mother in over three years. There was no way she would have called me, After all she did not know where to find my phone number.

"It couldn't have been. I'm sure it was my sister-in-law, trying to get to me." I doubted what my co-worker said and thought no more about it.

Later that afternoon, I answered my work phone and was surprised to hear a voice I had not heard in three years. Her first words were, "Let's let bygones be bygones and leave the past in the past." That was the greeting I received from my mother after all those years apart.

I poured my heart out, telling her what a mistake I had made. I was surprised at her willingness to assist me in getting out on my own. I began making plans and carving out my way.

Yet, I was about to hit another iceberg. My sister-in-law contacted me and would not let me go until I agreed to a meeting. I arrived with a heavy heart and a lot of prayer, but I bought into her lies that things would be different.

To the disbelief of my coworkers, I returned to my tumultuous home. The "things will be different" promise did not even last two days.

Two weeks later, we were out of town for a concert when my sister-in-law began arguing with me and reaching across the backseat to pull my hair. We were both adult women. She was old enough to be my mother, and we were acting like children.

My husband and brother-in-law found the solution by pulling off the road and putting me out on the side of the interstate. I was filled with anger and began to walk.

"Help me, Lord." I took a stupid risk and caught a ride with a stranger, but I can't help wondering in retrospect if God had sent me an angel. All of these years later, I wonder what would have happened if I had asked this stranger to take me to my mother.

Instead, like an idiot, I returned to our hotel room. When my husband, his sister and her husband returned that evening, they acted as if nothing happened.

From there the abuse escalated and grew more and more intense. The tension became so thick a knife would not have cut it. By Christmas day, we were not speaking to one another.

I was in a lifeboat that was limping along and I had no idea how to get out. I kept my newly established communication with my mother a secret, along with the fact we were working on a plan to get me out of this situation. I prayed that I could last a few more weeks, until Duncan and his sister would both be away on a planned trip.

Two days after Christmas, I was exhausted by the time I

returned home from work. Exhausted from the drama and never-ending rollercoaster. I lashed out when Duncan again mentioned all of the women in his life who wanted him.

"They can have you," I finally said. "I can't wait to leave you."

His eyes darkened to midnight black. "If you leave, my enemies will kill you." He reached up and attempted to choke me, as I fought to remove his fingers from around my throat. I'd heard these threats so many times they no longer had any effect on me.

"That's better than staying here with you. Maybe they will kill you instead." I slapped him on the cheek, as his sister stood back and cackled, before attempting another altercation.

Before the night ended, I was forcefully removed from the situation. As I spent the night in the police station, I wasn't sure whether to be worried about what would happen next or relieved to be out of the nightmare.

I spent the evening crying and praying, unsure of what to do. I was an emotional mess. I found a kindhearted officer who allowed me to call my mother and share with her what happened.

For the next five days, I waited and prayed. I had no idea what the future held, including where I would go when I left this holding place.

"For all I know, I'll be living on the street," I said to one woman who was also there.

I had to wait for the holiday and New Year to be over, but as I wept and prayed, I had no idea that a new beginning was awaiting me.

My mother arrived and I was released into her custody and care. A restraining order prevented all communication for a year between Duncan and me. However, that did not stop him from attempting to contact me and demanding to know where I was and when I was returning.

Rebuilding my life took years of work, counseling, forgiveness and peeling back the layers. Yet, this experience brought me much closer with both my Lord and Savior and my mother and siblings.

For the first time, I began to realize just how many people truly cared about me, loved me and had been praying for me during this perilous time in my life.

For three years, I had felt as if I were living on sinking sand. The abuse escalated so slowly that at first I did not realize I was in an abusive relationship. By the time I realized I was on the sinking ship there seemed no way out. When the abuse hit an all-time high, I felt as if I was sinking.

My lifeboat was my relationship with Jesus Christ. I had to turn the situation and all my hurt and pain over to him. I could not continue living that way and the entire situation seemed hopeless, but I knew that God loved me. I sought His will and way, because I knew He was the only one who could save me. Help did not arrive right away, but each day while I waited, I drew closer to my Lord.

I made my plans on how I would get away, but I also wavered, wondering if I would be strong enough to follow through. However, God showed up and provided a way, in a manner I never would have imagined.

The police responded to a call after an altercation. They removed me from the situation and I was reunited with Mama. All communication with my tormentors and abusers ended, and the healing process began.

I've discovered that when we place things in God's hands He never works the way we would imagine. Proverbs 3:5 tells us to "trust in the Lord with all your heart and lean not on your own understanding."

Regardless of your situation or the pain in your life, turn it over to Jesus. He will take it to work in ways you never fathomed.

3
Judy, Do You Trust Me?

Judith Victoria Hensley

I never thought I'd be included in the statistical count of failed marriages. Such a notion was nowhere in my scope of possibilities. As a preacher's kid who had been brought up to expect a life as wife, mother, and homemaker, with a possible career thrown in, I did not expect my marriage would crash and burn.

Young and naïve, I thought our marriage was truly made in heaven. I was told later on by a former classmate, "You two were the Barbie and Ken of campus! If you couldn't make it, what hope was there for the rest of us?"

The announcement came like a gunshot in the dark that struck my heart. "I love you, but I'm not in love with you," he said. "My happiness is all that matters."

These were words I never expected to hear. I wasn't even sure what they meant. How could I not have known that somewhere in the midst of things, the love switch had been flipped off on the other end while mine was still on?

It was a desperate time in my life. The apartment lease had been terminated and we had been in the process of buying a house. Bank account emptied, and only a small amount of money in my pocket, I headed north to my parents' home in a Chicago suburb. My family had not stopped loving me. I was blessed to have them and the church they pastored as a support group.

It was a season of needing kindness from people, but not wanting their pity. It was a span of time for needing help, but not wanting charity. It was a period when I was trying to see life as if peering through waxed paper. Nothing made any sense.

Even though doors had been opened to me and I could live with my family until I could earn enough money to move out, I felt that God had something more for me. My Heavenly Father had seen the train wreck in motion and knew all the details of what was going on, even though they were still hidden from me.

What should I do? Should I go? Should I stay? Should I get a job in a factory where I would make good wages? Should I try to work for the newspaper I had left years earlier? Should I return to college and become certified as a teacher?

My mind was a constant whirlpool of thoughts being sucked down into murky waters. I couldn't eat and didn't sleep. Each time the phone rang, I was sure someone on the other end was going to tell me it was all a mistake. Each time a car door slammed close to the house, I hoped there would be a knock on the door and I'd be taken back to our life and all the promises it held.

I learned what it meant to "pray without ceasing." Night and day, day and night, I bombarded heaven with prayers, asking for a miracle. I wasn't asking for God's will exactly. I knew God hated divorce, even though He loves divorced people. In my mind, God's will had to be that He would put Humpty Dumpty together again.

I have heard God speak directly into my soul on a few occasions. The Holy Spirit never says to me what I'm expecting or even hoping for. That particular day started out as all the days since I returned home. Then, I heard a question as loud and clear inside my heart as if someone was standing in the room speaking to me.

"Judy, do you trust me?"

"Yes, Lord," I answered.

I expected a dialogue, since the voice had been so clear, but nothing else came. I thought about what it meant to truly trust God in this situation. He was my only hope. I didn't realize that despite all my prayers and all my tears, I was still trying to convince God of what His will was in the circumstances.

A few hours passed, and the voice patiently asked me again, "Judy, do you trust me?"

"Yes, Lord," I answered again, convinced that I did.

No response.

Didn't God know I trusted him? Couldn't He see the inner workings of my heart and my mind? Didn't He know that I had loved him since I was a child? What exactly was He asking of me?

Several hours passed, then, "Judy, do you trust me?"

After milling it about all day in my head, I realized that God was requiring of me a more specific, more honest response.

"Lord, You know that I do. What do you want me to do?"

I did not get the answer I was hoping for. "Let go of everything."

What? What does that mean?

Okay . . . maybe it was a test and if I did let go of what I couldn't change, then . . . maybe God would force the other person to come back, fall in love again, and do my will.

My heart won out over my head. I loved God with all of my heart. He was asking me to walk on the water with Him, one step at a time. He was asking if I would continue to trust Him, even if things didn't play out as I hoped. He was asking me if I was willing to surrender myself and my logic into His loving hands. He was asking me to let go of trying to figure it all out and force the puzzle pieces into place.

I signed the papers for the house we were in the process of purchasing, releasing it into my husband's hands and put the papers in the mail that day. I never looked back. I never regretted doing what God had told me to do. I let go of everything.

That included the past. It included letting go of the man I loved who would soon take another woman in marriage. It included releasing the dreams of the future I had built around our marriage. I had to let go of the hurt and the anger that were like serpents knotted inside me. I had to let go of the fear that I could not raise an infant son on my own.

Letting go of everything did not happen instantly.

The process began when I chose to trust God for my life and my future, but letting go of everything covered a span of years before I was truly free.

Doors opened for me to return to college and get the teaching degree I had wanted. I recently retired after thirty years in the classroom and continue as an after-school tutor. My son is a successful adult with two beautiful children. My life did not turn out to be the one I had dreamed of or had planned. It is different but has been rich and rewarding all along the way and filled with opportunities and adventures I didn't anticipate. With God's help, I've navigated them all.

My Father had asked me, "Judy, do you trust me?"

My answer then and now, and every single day is still, "Yes, Lord. I do."

4

An Angel by My Side

Lola Di Giulio De Maci

My husband and I had been married forty-seven years when I got the call from the hospital. "I'm sorry," someone said in a steady, even voice. "He didn't make it."

I sat at the other end of the line, feeling my heart begin to break. "He didn't make it," a voice inside me kept repeating. It was Sunday. November 1, 2015. All Saints' Day.

The next morning I set about making plans for the funeral. My husband had mentioned more than once that he wanted to be buried at the veterans' cemetery among those men and women who had served their country.

"I will honor your wishes," I assured him.

On the morning before Veterans Day, my children and I and a few friends gathered at the cemetery, waiting for the Navy to tell us where to go for the burial. I had never been to a military funeral before. We followed the procession to a sunny spot surrounded by manicured lawns and tall trees. In this hallowed space, military honors would be bestowed on a dedicated Navy Chief who, decades earlier, was a young sailor ready and willing to serve his country. The bright morning sun illuminated the colors of the flag draping the casket, making the red, white, and blue more vibrant, alive, and meaningful. My heart overflowed with pride.

At the opening of the ceremony, two Seamen reverently lifted the flag from its place on the casket and, from one to the other, meticulously folded the length of the flag into a perfect triangle. They handed the flag to the Chief who, in turn, knelt at my feet and placed the flag into my hands.

"Thank you. It's beautiful," I whispered, looking into the face of this young man who was honoring his fallen older brother. I clutched the flag to my chest, embracing its beauty and spirit . . . until it was time to go.

I have taken great solace in the flag that was presented to me on that solemn day. This priceless keepsake is displayed in a United States Navy flag case and sits on my hearth next to a statue of a Bereavement Angel that my cousin had sent me shortly after Bernard's passing. The angel's arms are outstretched toward heaven, and she is holding a lone star in her hands. The message written in the folds of her skirt reads, "Perhaps they are not stars but rather openings where our loved ones shine down to let us know they are happy."

Last fall, I was shopping for Christmas gifts, and I found the website that offered the Bereavement Angel along with a variety of other angels. I had just placed my order for a Hope Angel for my niece and a Comfort Angel for a friend when a Military Angel appeared on my computer screen. She was dressed simply in blue and white, clutching the American flag to her chest, the flag folded in a perfect triangle. A price was listed, as well as a brief description. I immediately dialed the toll-free number noted at the top of the screen, as the site I was browsing did not offer this angel.

"I have to have that Military Angel!" I said to the representative who answered the call. I'm sure she detected the urgency in my voice.

"We only have a few left in stock," she said. "I'll see what I can do. It will probably take two to three weeks before you receive it."

A couple of days later, on November 1, 2016, the first anniversary of my husband's passing, this Military Angel appeared on my computer screen when I opened my laptop. Just a picture of her. Spanning the screen. No words. No price. Just her. In a field of blue. I hadn't even signed in yet.

Two days after that, the angel appeared on the screen again, before I logged in. She didn't stay long. Just long enough to have said, "Hi! I'm here," and leave. What was she trying to tell me?

The next evening my daughter stopped by. I had told her about "my angel."

"Want to see a picture of her?"

I opened my laptop and a message appeared on the screen that I had never seen before: *This page is having trouble loading.* I clicked on the red x in the upper right-hand corner several times, but I couldn't delete the message. I was about to give up when the message disappeared. In its place, the angel appeared.

"It's her!" I cried. "She's here again!"

"Mom, this is a sign! I think Dad is trying to tell you something."

On the morning of November 8, 2016, the package containing the Military Angel appeared on my doorstep. I carefully unwrapped the package and placed the angel on the hearth next to the American flag and the Bereavement Angel.

On Veterans Day, November 11th, we would be commemorating and honoring all those men and women who served their country in the name of peace and freedom. And I would be honoring and remembering a young, zealous sailor who came into my life fifty years ago.

Suddenly, a voice inside my heart said, "Everything is going to be all right."

And I knew it would be.

5

The Treasure

Robert W. Rettie

Our new home was an army post on the Philippine Island of Luzon. Dad, a captain in the army, was assigned to Luzon in 1946, the year after World War II ended. Mom and I followed him in early 1947. What happened on that island would affect me and my friends for the rest of our lives.

One hot afternoon my fifth-grade classmate, Porky, and I were sitting in my front yard trying to think of something to do with our unexpected day off. Although unexpected, canceled classes were not unusual.

Our elementary school was located on a World War II battle site. Construction had been completed before this was discovered. On occasion, one of us kids would go into the classroom after recess with a handful of unexploded bullets we had discovered on the playground. The teachers would run around frantically, yelling and ringing alarm bells. It was fun to watch.

Then, students would be dismissed as soldiers formed a long line and patrolled the playground, picking up various objects considered dangerous.

Once they determined the area was safe, we returned to school. Everything went back to normal — until the next cache was discovered.

Sometimes a student saved a few bullets instead of giving all of them to the teacher; then brought them in on a day a test was scheduled. The teachers soon caught on to the charade but they couldn't take chances. The test would be postponed and school dismissed for the rest of the day. The hot afternoon Porky and I were sitting in my front yard was one of those days.

"We could hike out to the firing range," I suggested to Porky.

"Maybe one of the soldiers will let us shoot a rifle like they did last time." Then I remembered the trouble that caused my dad.

"No! We better not do that again," I commented. "We could walk to the Post Exchange to see if there are any new comic books."

Porky's mouth began moving. No sound. It took him awhile to get started and even longer to get the words out. Porky stuttered. Some days, depending on circumstances, he could stutter like a machine gun. That's how he got his nickname. All of us guys that hung out together had nicknames. Porky considered his the best because he was named after his favorite cartoon character, Porky Pig.

While I waited for him to decide what we should do, I heard the bike of our friend, Billy. Billy had about a thousand playing cards pinned between the spokes of his bike. He could be heard a mile away. He rode up, slid to a stop, and jumped off. He could hardly wait to show Porky and me what he found.

"Look at this," Billy said, as he held out both hands. We had no idea what he was holding. It didn't look like anything that should make him that excited. It was just a metal box.

"I think it's some kind of secret treasure," Billy said. "I'm going to open it. I bet there's money or something really neat inside." He paused for a moment. "Can either of you guys get a hammer or screwdriver?"

I knew where my dad kept his hammer. We went into my house. I handed the hammer to Billy. His excitement increased. "OK! Let's go back outside and get this thing open."

As we were running down the front steps of our porch, we heard Billy's mom call him. They lived a few houses away.

He took the hammer from me. "Sorry! I gotta go, but when I get home I'm gonna get this thing open." He grinned. "I can't wait to see what's inside. I'll bring the hammer back tomorrow and show you what I find." He jumped on his bike and was gone in a roar of flapping playing cards.

"That Billy sure is lucky," I told Porky. "I wish we could find something neat like that. Did he tell you where he found it?"

Porky told me that Billy found the box that morning on the school playground.

Just then we heard a loud explosion and felt the ground tremble. Large plumes of dark smoke rose from Billy's backyard. The air was suddenly filled with the sound of frightened voices calling children to return home. Mothers heard and felt the explosion. They knew it was time for a head count.

Billy and his younger sister were killed in the explosion. The "treasure" was a forgotten Japanese land mine.

A few days later Dad came into my bedroom, holding his open toolbox.

"Son," he said, "have you seen my hammer?"

I had never lied to my dad. I hesitated before answering. I finally said, "I gave it to Billy." I looked down at the floor and waited for his response.

"I know Billy was your friend. I'm sorry, Son," he said as he touched my shoulder. "I'm sure there's another hammer around here somewhere. Why don't you help me look for it?"

It took a long while before my buddies and I could return to our fun-loving activities, and there were differences. There were fewer incidents of unexploded bullets brought into the classroom, and if we found something out of the ordinary on the playground, we let one of the soldiers determine if it might be dangerous.

We never knew for sure why the landmine exploded the day Billy and his sister died. We only knew Billy told us he planned on using the hammer to pry open the box he was positive held a treasure.

As I grew and matured, I never forgot about Billy. I knew him for a long time, and I knew about his faithfulness to church. He never missed a Sunday school class. Though he did not find the treasure he was looking for here on earth, I know Billy found it in Heaven.

6

The Belonging Hand

Sharon Frazier

Have you ever had an epiphany? I believe I had an experience when God unexpectedly dropped a full-blown object lesson into my mind and soul. He interrupted my ordinary routine with an extraordinary insight that answered many questions I had and deepened my relationship with Him. God gave me an epiphany during a simple interaction with my then five-year-old daughter.

"Mama?" Karen asked. "Can I go play with Eric?"

"I'll call Eric's mother and see if it's okay," I told her. I called and Abby assured me it was fine for Karen to come over.

"Hold Mama's hand," I said. Karen gave me her hand, and we walked to the end of our driveway as a line of cars came around the corner. Waiting for a chance to cross the street, I glanced at her small hand clasped in mine. That picture sent a flood of thoughts cascading through my mind. *She completely trusts me to know when to go. She doesn't run ahead of me. She looks to me for provision and protection. She accepts her dependence on me. She doesn't question her place as my daughter.*

At times I have questioned my place as God's daughter. I have agonized over whether I had the right motives for following him, and not only for what he could give me. But as I reflected about Karen's innocent dependence on me, I was struck with a new possibility.

Could it be that God does not disapprove of our need for him, and what he can give us? I thought of Psalm 103:13-14 (NLT) that tells us *the Lord is like a father to his children, tender and compassionate to those who fear him. For he understands how weak we are; he knows we are only dust.* God knows my need for provision, for acceptance, for everything that he is. I finally understood that coming to God, accepting my need for what he can give me is what pleases him most.

I didn't consider Karen as selfish for her dependence on me. I cared for her and watched over her because she was my beloved daughter. Could I have that same assurance of belonging in God's family? Romans 8:14-15 NLT tells us *all who are led by the Spirit of God are children of God. . . . You should behave like God's very own children, adopted into his family – calling him "Father, dear Father."* I began to grasp that God welcomes me like a little child, taking my hand in his great big hand.

I wondered if that's how it was in the Garden of Eden before the fall — Adam and Eve enjoying unself-conscious fellowship with God and acknowledging God as their Creator and Sustainer?

I'm overwhelmed that God stepped out of the distant pages of the Bible and into my daily life. I'm convinced that when I wasn't even looking for it, God gave me this experience to teach me to see him as my Father, and for me to come to him as his child.

And to think . . . I learned this lesson from the ordinary sight of my little girl's hand in mine. Now I place my hand in His.

7

Landstuhl — We've Got an Emergency!

Lt. Col. Robert B. Robeson (USAF Retired)

And they came to Him (Jesus) and woke Him up, saying, "Master, Master, we are perishing!" And being aroused, He rebuked the wind and the surging waves, and they stopped and became calm. And He said to them (His disciples), "Where is your faith?"
Luke 8:24-25 NAS

It was cool and peaceful that fall morning in 1972 at the 63rd Medical Detachment (Helicopter Ambulance) heliport outside Landstuhl, West Germany. The night's dew still glistened on runway grass and beaded like tiny crystals on the concrete beneath the aircraft where my copilot Stu, a fellow captain, and I were preflighting. Two of our five UH-1H ("Huey") medical evacuation helicopters were down for maintenance and we were preparing to fly to our maintenance unit at Mannheim, next to the Rhine River, to pick up the necessary parts.

The weather forecaster had given me good flight information but had noted in the remarks section of the flight plan that a front was moving in from France and we could expect heavy fog and rain later that morning.

We were both a couple years out of Vietnam, had been shot up or shot down there by enemy fire twelve times — seven of them mine — and had accumulated nearly 3,000 flight hours between us. Flying over West Germany, Belgium and Luxembourg, there had often been discussions between us of a religious nature. Stu respected Christianity but wasn't an active Christian. He'd smiled when I related my feelings to him about the two times I'd been shot down in Southeast Asia in 1969. I'd told him I knew, without a doubt, that God was the only reason I was still alive. My father, a Protestant minister, had raised my brother and me with the knowledge and understanding that believing and having faith in Jesus for what He had accomplished on the cross for our sins was what is most essential, regardless of any situation we would ever find ourselves in.

"Yeah, I know, John told me."

CW2 John Ball (nicknamed Eight Ball) was a crusty older warrant officer from our former unit, the 236th Medical Detachment in Da Nang, South Vietnam, who had taught me a great deal about combat flying. I was his copilot the first time I was shot down and he'd managed to arrange for me to be stationed with him again, this time in Europe, eight months after he'd left our unit on December 15, 1969 en route to his next duty station in Landstuhl. His wife, Rose, was born in West Germany. He'd met and married her on an earlier tour of duty there.

In Mannheim we had to wait longer than anticipated while a special part was located. The weather didn't cross my mind until we were airborne again.

"Landstuhl, this is Army 7-4-2. How's the weather?" Stu radioed.

"Fog's lying in heavy now, 7-4-2. That front is here already. Better hurry."

"Roger that. We're about twenty minutes out."

The sky had darkened and patches of fog were beginning to swirl below. A few minutes went by.

"Do you smell hydraulic fluid?" I asked Stu.

"Yeah, I sure do. I checked the reservoir on preflight and it was right on the mark."

In an instant, a sinking sensation gripped my chest. The yellow master caution light on the instrument panel had been activated by an emergency condition. I glanced down at the pedestal between us and the emergency panel hydraulic light told me what I already knew from the feedback in my controls. They'd become so heavy that it felt as if they'd been welded to the aircraft frame. *There was a leak somewhere in the system.*

Even though we practiced this emergency maneuver often, putting a sick bird down in crummy weather on an enclosed site the size of our heliport — that had 30-foot trees on four sides and only about one-eighth of a mile of grass runway — wasn't at the top of my "wish list."

I said a quick, silent prayer for our safety as we hurried through our emergency procedures. When we'd finished, Stu called the heliport."Landstuhl, 7-4-2 again. We've got an emergency."

John, who was also our unit training and standardization pilot, took over the FM radio from the enlisted radio operator. "Say emergency, 7-4-2."

"Lost our hydraulics," Stu said matter-of-factly "We've gone through all of the emergency procedures. No go."

"State your intentions."

I keyed the mike switch on my cyclic control stick, the steering wheel of our aircraft. "John, I'll try to bring it in there at home base."

At that moment, something else hit us. Fog! It wasn't thick enough then to go on instruments, but I knew we were pushing the trouble envelope. Trees were barely visible along the ridgeline where the heliport should have been. I made a slow descent, feeling for some attachment with the earth and lined up where I hoped the runway would be. Suddenly we broke through the fog and clouds at 80 knots and I saw concrete flying by beneath my feet through my chin bubble . . . then grass.

"7-4-2, make a go-around. Go around!" John directed forcefully.

It took all of my strength to move the pedals, collective control, and the cyclic stick to compensate for the added power to make a go-around. I was sweating, tired, and for the first time, anxious.

"Stu, I'm going on instruments. You stay outside and let me know when you can see the ground."

"Right."

I climbed a few hundred feet into the damp, dreary whiteness and flew in a flat left-hand turn, hoping to find enough clear air to land. Without hydraulics we'd have to make a running landing with our skids and allow the ground run to stop our momentum. This procedure would relieve us from having to move the controls any more than necessary. The fog and clouds were just an added misery and nuisance that had the potential to cause more havoc . . . or create a messy Huey sandwich atop a ridge that had been a part of the Siegfried Line during WWII.

Lining up again with where I believed the ridgeline was, I began decreasing my airspeed. We descended a few feet at a time, attempting to pick up the dark silhouette of the trees below. I offered up another silent prayer that I can still recall to this day. "Lord, you can allow this landing to be really hairy, but please don't let it be impossible."

"I've got ground," Stu alerted me, over the intercom, a few seconds later.

Glancing up from the needles and gauges, I observed a thin corridor of light in the fog the width of our cabin and at about a 45-degree angle to the runway. In seconds, we were again whizzing by the concrete landing pad.

"7-4-2, you're too fast. Make another go-around," John repeated.

It was at that moment when I felt a sudden calmness come over my spirit. "No! Let's put it down now, Stu."

As if we'd practiced together for years, I felt Stu come on the controls. Not once did he move against me. Within seconds our skids touched down awkwardly, but efficiently, as fog swirled up around our Plexiglas windows. We slid for what seemed like a lifetime on the grass beyond the concrete landing pad before coming to a stop. Thirty feet away from our still spinning main rotor blades stood trees — dark shadows in the fog — marking the end of our heliport's grass runway.

Stu reached over and grasped my hand in an unusual gesture of emotion for him.

"He was flying with us today, wasn't He, buddy?"

I took a deep breath, nodded, and throttled back to "flight idle," to allow our Lycoming jet engine to cool for a required two minutes, before shutting down. Then I sat there in quiet meditation, giving the butterflies in my stomach a chance to settle. Seconds later, an ambulance and fire truck came screaming alongside, sirens shrieking and red lights flashing.

In Operations, I hung my flight gear in my locker. Then I turned and grinned in John's direction. In that instant of awareness we both remembered another time, on September 13, 1969 in Southeast Asia, when he had been wounded in the leg and I somehow managed to get our bullet-riddled bird to earth in one piece. That time, coincidentally, he had been the one to say "Someone else was flying with us today."

"Give me a break," I said to John. "A fire truck and ambulance? I thought you taught me how to fly the tough ones."

John's craggy face wrinkled and he almost cracked a smile. Even from across the room I could see moisture in his eyes. "Christian," he said, using the nickname my fellow pilots had given me in Vietnam, "as soon as the weather clears, we gotta work on your emergency hydraulics-off procedure. That had to be the sorriest landing I've ever seen."

Now, 49 years later, Genesis 18:14 (KJV) still filters through my mind. "*Is anything too hard for the Lord?*" As confirmed in that Landstuhl, West Germany flight — and so many times before and after during those 19 years in U.S. Army aviation — this question had already been answered. All we had needed was a little "light." I believe, because of my faith in God, He had provided it to me both materially and spiritually. What more could a pilot or person ask for than that?

8

Sufficient Grace

Bobbie Ann DuPree Foshee

"You have breast cancer." It's a diagnosis every woman fears. The words bounced around inside my head, colliding with every nerve of my body. They settled in my heart. That was not what I expected to hear and not at all what I *wanted* to hear.

My journey began with a routine mammogram on November 10, 2015, followed by three biopsies the next week. The results were anything but routine. At first, the diagnosis was grade three cancer, so I was sent to an oncologist and a surgeon. They ordered an MRI and a PET scan ASAP. The results came three days before Christmas: worse than expected — stage four.

I left that appointment in shock, yet determined. I knew I couldn't endure what was to come on my own, so I contacted the prayer warriors in my life.

My pastor-son and his wife began to pray immediately. I called family and friends who put me on more prayer chains than I thought possible. As word spread, my name was on the lips of people all over the world, asking God to heal my body. My church family gathered around and anointed me with oil as we stood in agreement that this would be defeated in Jesus' name. My sister, a writer, asked the prayer warriors she knew in the Christian writing community to pray for me. I knew I was in good hands . . . God's hands.

In early January, 2016, the first of many chemo treatments began. The idea was to shrink the tumors as much as possible prior to surgery, thus giving the surgeon a better chance at removing most, if not all, of the diseased tissues. The chemo treatments took about six hours each time as they were giving me four different drugs. I had those treatments every twenty-one days. All possible side effects bombarded my body. Except one.

Most people get nausea, but I was blessed in having very little. I wrote in my journal, "Praise the Lord for that! I am clinging to my Rock of Ages." Although I didn't experience a lot of nausea, the chemo completely wiped me out. I could barely stand. In three weeks' time, I lost thirty pounds. Now, I didn't mind the weight loss, but this isn't the way I would have planned it.

Life was getting more complicated by my illness. In March of 2015, my husband had his fourth stroke. This one left him unable to perform everyday tasks. He relied on me. For everything. My family and I knew the day would come when I would no longer be able to care for my beloved husband. In January, 2016 we made the heartbreaking decision to place him into an assisted-living facility.

A year later, I underwent surgery to remove my right breast and eleven lymph nodes. It was hard, but with God's help, I pressed on.

March 26 was our 54th wedding anniversary. I was extremely depressed. We'd both been through so much and instead of being with one another and being the bulwark we had expected to be, he was in one place and I in another. That wasn't a good day.

The next day was Easter Sunday. With a lot of help from family, I was able to attend church for the first time in months. While there, a feeling of joy and peace came upon me. I felt as if my burdens were lifted. My burdens were nothing when compared to what Jesus had done for me on the cross. That day — things turned around.

I began to try to go upstairs where our kitchen is located. It was excruciating . . . two steps up, stop to catch my breath, then go again. Eventually, I was able to ascend those stairs without having to stop.

April brought a new round of battles. I finished three of the drugs in my chemo cocktail, but I began the first of what would be fifty-five radiation treatments. During those treatments I hummed hymns to keep my mind off what my body was having to endure. I hummed "Blessed Assurance," "The King is Coming," "I Surrender All," and one of my favorites sung in my daughter's Messianic Church, "La Dor Vador."

By June I was given the green light to go on a family vacation.

Fifteen of us traveled to North Carolina for some much-needed time away. Joy filled my heart at seeing my grandchildren and my great-granddaughter splash away in the pool. Their laughter was music to my soul.

By July I began to get around far better. I could finally work with my flowers, amaryllis and daylilies, a legacy from my daddy. I even cooked a bit for the family.

I was told in November that I had to have one final PET scan at the end of December. That scan would determine my future. Our son picked up my husband from the assisted-living facility and brought him home for Thanksgiving. It was a great day as we were together, surrounded by our children, grandchildren, and great-grandchildren.

On December 29th I met with my oncologist for the results of the PET scan. He picked up the report, looked it over, and shook his head.

I thought, *Oh, no.*

He looked up at me and said, "Mrs. Foshee . . . you are cancer free." My ears could hardly believe his words, but my heart and my spirit already knew it was so.

Thanks to doctors who refused to stop treatments, to countless people the world over who prayed for me, to my Jesus who suffered the scourge of the stripes upon his body for me . . . *I am healed.*

Each day I have left upon this earth is more precious than the one before. I treasure every single day, trusting and knowing that God has everything under control. From before I was born, He knew the number of my days. He knew the battle I would face, but He was in the middle of it with me.

I've lived to see four more great-grands born into our family, and two more are due this year. Blessings continue to pour upon me and my family. What an awesome God we serve!

I wrote in my journal, "I continue to thank you, Jesus, for what you have done already and I thank you for what you are continuing to do."

His grace is sufficient for me.

9

Looking for the Rainbow

Judith Vander Wege

The Bible contains many wonderful promises. I've often wondered — Do these all apply to me?

For many years, I had a bumper sticker on my car that said, "God keeps his promises." The background was a picture of a rainbow. Sometimes when I washed the car, I could see a real rainbow in the clean, wet windows. It happened when I stood a certain way with my back to the sun.

This taught me that just as I needed to stand in a certain position to see the rainbow in the car windows, so also I need to live in a certain position with God before I can receive his promises. To get right with him, I need to search my heart to identify my sin, confess it, receive forgiveness, and turn away from it. Since then, I pray for constant guidance and the ability to obey, living and walking in that right relationship with my heavenly Father.

At certain times, especially after a rainstorm, rainbows are in the sky for everyone to see. But to appropriate God's promises, we need to fit into his plans. His plans for us are for good, not for evil. He won't force us to fit into his plans, but we can get into the right relationship with him through believing in Jesus Christ and receiving him as Savior and LORD. Then we will obey him, thus being in the right position to receive his promises — a rainbow of blessings.

10

My Husband Gave Me 30 Days

Sheryl Boldt

Bert had never come home in the middle of a workday, but six years ago, on April 1, he did, and said, "We need to talk."

I was curious and a little excited about whatever he wanted to discuss. Did he have news about our plans for building our beach house? Or maybe he'd found someone to buy his business so he could semi-retire. Nothing could have prepared me for the next words out of his mouth.

"I want a divorce."

His words sliced through me, and a hard knot formed in the pit of my stomach. I could tell from the look on his face that this was no April Fool's joke.

Bert stood in our den and counted on his fingers the reasons he could no longer tolerate being married to me. "I'm tired of your nagging, Sheryl! I'm sick of hearing what I should eat or how much I should read my Bible." His voice grew louder as he continued, "And I'm tired of trying to follow all the rules. Good gosh, Sheryl, what does it matter if the silverware faces up or down in the dishwasher? And I don't want to squeegee the shower door every time I shower. Give me a break!"

Every time he listed another reason, the knot in my stomach grew. He ended with words no spouse ever wants to hear. "I'm through with this marriage."

He waited for me to respond, but I couldn't speak. My face turned hot, and my eyes filled with tears. Unable to meet his angry glare, I stared at my lap until I could find my voice. I knew I couldn't deny his charges. Although I'd been praying for God to change me, I was indeed guilty of nagging and trying to control Bert. Finally, I said, "Bert, you're right."

He lowered himself into his favorite recliner and leaned forward. In a kinder tone, he told me his plan. We would stay in our house, but in separate bedrooms, for one month. During that time, I was to find an apartment near my children in Louisiana.

Suddenly, the talk was over. “Don’t wait up for me,” he said as he stalked toward the door.

I heard the garage door close, and I gave in to tears — and panic. As the reality of what had just happened began to sink in, I became less worried about what would become of me and more worried about what I had become.

I knew Bert was right. For some time I’d noticed how critical and angry I’d been. The more he put his work and his needs ahead of mine and our relationship, the worse my behavior became. I felt rejected, and I wasn’t shy about letting him know how I felt.

I began to question my behavior as a Christian — an imitator of Christ. Justified or not, this was not the kind of person I wanted to be. But after so many years, was it possible to change? Since my first marriage had ended in divorce, I feared that if I didn’t get it right this time, I could never again trust myself to marry.

And now I had thirty days to become the wife I desperately wanted to be. Although I knew I wasn’t completely responsible for our problems, I felt the weight of the wrongs I had committed against Bert.

God, please change me! I cried.

When Bert came home late that evening, I asked if I could speak with him. Crossing his arms, he said coldly, “Yes, but I’ve made up my mind. I want a divorce.”

Tears filled my eyes, but I pressed on. “Bert, I know I’ve messed up. I’m asking for a second chance. I’m not asking you to change. Right now, let me do all the changing.” I was shocked to hear those words coming out of my mouth. Obviously God was already at work.

“I don’t care how much you change,” he said. “I’m not changing my mind.”

"Okay, but I'm still going to try."

The next day, I searched my bookshelves for Dr. Emerson Eggerichs' book, *Love & Respect: The Love She Most Desires, The Respect He Desperately Needs*. It had been sitting there, unread for years. Next to it sat R.T. Kendall's book, *Total Forgiveness*, and I pulled that down as well.

One morning I opened *Love & Respect* and read testimonies from women who described their disrespectful behavior toward their husbands. Ashamed, I saw myself in many of their stories. *Oh, God, no wonder our marriage has gotten so bad!* The more I read, the more I saw how my constant criticism and disrespectful tone had undermined my husband.

Kendall's words reminded me of the rewards for totally forgiving those who hurt us. And he reminded me that I, too, needed mercy and forgiveness. I cried into my hands as I repented again for my angry, spiteful, and self-righteous heart. Before the day ended, I'd made scripture memory cards with verses on forgiveness.

To my sorrow, my repentant ways seemed to have no effect on Bert.

As I continued to read and practice the principles in Eggerich's and Kendall's books, I began to behave and think differently. Instead of nagging Bert to eat healthily, I bought food I knew he liked. Instead of lecturing him about going to church or having a quiet time, I held my tongue and prayed for him. And though I had always had a difficult time keeping up with the house, I made an extra effort to keep it neat and tidy. When he came home, later and later each night, I made sure I looked pretty.

With God's help, I chose to forgive Bert for his failures and continued to take responsibility for mine. I didn't do everything right, and sometimes I would slip back into my bad habits, but my repentance was real. I prayed constantly and kept my scripture memory cards nearby so I could meditate on them throughout the day.

God's presence continued to penetrate my sadness, even at night — especially the nights I cried alone in our bed. But my hope was growing. I began to understand that my significance was in Jesus, not in Bert's opinion of me. Because of this dawning awareness, I was better able to resist temptation and behave like the wife Bert thought he had married.

Sadly, Bert continued with his plans for divorce. As my 30-day deadline drew near, I knew I had to begin making plans. I had resisted calling family and friends, but now it was time to make some phone calls.

I picked up the phone. "Bert, I'm going to call my sisters so they can help me pack. . ." My voice choked, and I broke into sobs. "But I'm so disappointed because I really wanted things to work out."

Bert sat up in his chair, "Wait! What are you doing?"

"I'm calling Karen."

"Why?"

"Because the month is almost up. You wanted me out by the 30th."

"Wait. Let's talk about this."

Startled, I put down the phone. "I don't understand." Afraid to hope, I held my breath and waited.

Tears formed in his eyes. "Sheryl, I've never had anyone love me like you do. I've never had someone who was willing to stay with me in spite of my selfish, self-centered behavior." He pulled me closer to him. "Will you forgive me?"

I couldn't believe what I was hearing. I covered my mouth with my hands and laughed — and cried! *Is this really happening?*

Bert walked to the guest room and came back holding his wedding ring. He slid it onto his finger and said, "I'll never take it off again." More tears filled his eyes. "I've been a fool. I want to ask you to give me and our marriage another chance."

I buried my face in his shoulder, trying to control my crying. But this time, it was a good kind of crying. *Thank You, Father.*

"I know I've been distant and not there for you. I'm sorry."

"Oh, Bert. I'm sorry, too, for the ways I've been treating you.

I will honestly try to be more respectful — even when you're not perfect." We both chuckled through our tears.

My husband pulled me toward him again, and we held each other for a long, long while. What an incredible turn around — due to an incredible God. My heart swelled with thankfulness as I continued with my silent praise to a God who had given me the second chance I asked for.

Bert and I are thankful for all God has done in our marriage, but we candidly admit we are still a work in progress. We are, however, pleased to report: forgiving, loving, and respecting each other is much easier today than when our journey first began.

11

Unpredictable, Like Cloudbursts

Susan Boskat Murray

"This is the spot, right?" I looked to my husband, Murray, for confirmation.

"Yes!" chimed in five-year old Brent. "Look at all the *rocks!*" Murray hoisted up three-year-old Bryce and reached his hand out to Brent. I drew closer to the trio with eighteen-month-old Bradfield on my hip, and we bowed our heads in prayer. This was the spot.

Although I was apprehensive about taking the giant financial leap of building a new home, the steadfast heart of our kindergartner completely humbled me. Brent totally entrusted the future to God based on his understanding of the wise man who built his house on the rock.

Before leaving the site that day, Murray and I created an object lesson at the stone-laden little brook that ran through the back of the property. The rocks couldn't be broken, they didn't dissolve or float away, and the larger ones couldn't even be moved — characteristics of an all-powerful God. Among the specimens that we examined for strength, durability, and imperviousness was the most unique composite I had ever seen. I snatched up that three-dimensional, five-pound jigsaw puzzle as a tangible reminder of God's provision. It found a permanent home, covering a spare house key on a large wooden planter box just outside the garage patio of our new residence. In no way could I have imagined how the house on the rock story would become my own.

Things went well for us, and as the years passed, that little rock became a symbol of God's blessings — especially the time we were locked out in a snowstorm. We also had devotions out back in nice weather, and it was astounding as to how many of those lessons mentioned a rock.

One rainy summer night, however, Murray and I groggily awakened in the wee hours to a thunderous roar. Peering out our second-story bedroom window in the darkness, we were stunned to discover that our house was engulfed by torrents of water. The tiny creek had turned into a raging river and was swallowing us.

"The rabbits!" Immediately thinking of the pets in the basement, Murray rushed downstairs as I awakened the kids to pray.

"It's safe," Murray said from a dry concrete floor. "But we need to get the rabbits to higher ground. Those doors won't hold much longer."

The walk-out basement, with two sliding glass doors, served as a convenient, secure place to house the bunnies at night. At that moment, there was approximately eighteen inches of water gushing against the double panes. We had little time before the mounting pressure would explode the glass and force a tidal wave into the entire basement. We quickly scrambled to hustle anything of value out of danger. Although it seemed to last forever, within a half hour the water began to subside. The doors held — and God had miraculously provided a sanctuary for the bunnies.

Later that morning, we learned that a town-wide "cloudburst" had inundated homes in the hilly landscape for several miles around. One man, a half mile up an adjoining road, told us that he had come home from work at 3:00 A.M. to find his barn submerged in three feet of water.

Another was shocked to learn that his ten by twelve-foot tool shed had been deposited in a neighbor's yard. Everyone was discarding drenched furniture, carpets, and miscellany from their flooded basements — everyone except us. One neighbor actually commented that it was like the parting of the Red Sea. Our house, which was right at a natural turning point of the ravaging flow, should have seen the most damage. Instead, the deluge had literally split and left only minor seepage through our glass basement doors.

Outside, things were not so pretty. At the stream's pivot, our yard had collected an abundance of debris that washed down with the storm. The kids' free-standing, five-hundred-pound wooden playhouse had been relocated fifty feet from where it had been, and we never did find the outdoor wooden rabbit hutch. The patio had also been swept clean of a metal table, chairs, and the large wooden planter box that held the rock. The rock, our rock, was gone.

It took us two full days to clean up and dispose of the branches and trash on our property. Exhausted and relieved when things were finally back to normal, we again thanked God for minimal loss. Not surprisingly, it was Brent who mentioned the rock.

"I'm sorry, Brent," I said sadly. "It's gone."

"No, it's not," said Murray. He disappeared into the garage and returned as quickly as he had entered it.

"Things were so crazy," he said, "that I forgot to tell you." I stood there with my mouth hanging open as he handed me the rock!

"You *forgot* to tell me?" I said. "Where did you find it?"

"On the ground, right where the box used to be," he said. "It was wedged against the door jamb."

I was dumbfounded. Items that had been bigger, heavier, and more firmly anchored had been whooshed away by the current. But other than falling to the ground, the rock had not moved from its original position.

Over the past twenty years (and three houses), life has been unpredictable — just like cloudbursts. Having to sell our dream home due to a layoff was one of several rainfalls on the path of our lives. But throughout them all, I have carried that rock — and The Rock has carried me. Building my house on the firm foundation of Jesus doesn't mean I won't experience floods, droughts, tornadoes, tremors, or eruptions. It does mean, however, that I will not be shattered. I will not dissolve or be washed away because He is the hope that overcomes the cloudbursts in my life. And I have the rock to prove it!

12

A Tragic Day

Jonathan Hayashi

August 19, 2013 was a normal Monday in the office at Uptown Baptist Church in Chicago. Regular employees were working and interacting with one another; no one would have thought it would be such a tragic day.

I went through my regular routine of administration tasks and working on the service sermon prep for the soup kitchen ministry. The service began at 5:00 P.M. and we welcomed the one-hundred-fifty people from the streets into the first service. We began our second service and had approximately one hundred people in the pews waiting to hear the sermon. I got into the pulpit and began to preach.

It was 6:00 P.M. when we heard bang, bang, bang . . . about twenty loud bangs that sounded like fireworks! I turned around. "It's just fireworks, folks. Don't worry. Have a seat."

One of our deacons said, "No, I know that was not fireworks. It was too loud for it to be fireworks and it was real close."

I could feel the tension in the air and the noise shook me at the core of my inner being. The adrenaline rushed through my veins and my heart was pounding. I rushed to the church steps and burst through the doors. There it was — chaos! It looked like war had taken place. It was a drive-by shooting. People were running in every direction, hundreds of tormented souls on the streets, children screaming and howling. Shattered glass, bullet shells on the ground, people fighting and yelling.

At the church steps, I recognized two young men on the ground. The face of one was planted in a pool of blood. The other one had multiple bullet holes in his body.

"Pastor, I just got shot in my legs," said a man who had gone through the earlier service. Another man had been shot in his thigh, and another in his wrist. I looked at the twenty-one-year-old boy with a bullet hold in his head, seeing his brain burst out like Jell-o.

I dialed 911. "My name is Jonathan Hayashi, we had a shooting at 1011 West Wilson Avenue."

As I was explaining, two police vehicles came from the south and an ambulance came from west of Wilson. Police officers were running across the streets; yellow tape was put around the crosswalk to secure the area. I stood there in silence, not knowing what to do, simply being in the midst of the tragedy that took place at our church steps.

"Why, God?"

As I looked back at my past, I knew I could easily have been one of a different group.

I vividly recalled the day when I saw in the newspaper that my eighteen-year-old friend had died in gang activity. That could have been me, if I had stayed in the gang.

But I had met Christ. I knew God loved me and had a plan for my life.

My thoughts turned to the kids running around the streets of Chicago killing one another.

I've learned a few things from God protecting me from destruction.

Life has meaning.

Life is short and precious.

Our purpose is for the kingdom of God.

God has created us in His image and loves us. He loves us so much he sent his son, Jesus, so that whoever believes in Him shall never perish, but have everlasting life that is the greatest.

It is the gospel.

The message of biblical Christianity is not, "God loves me, period."

It is, "God loves me so that I might make him, his way, his salvation, his glory, and his greatness known among all nations, and among our neighbors."

I have learned and seen firsthand that people are dying without having heard the gospel. I've heard the term, "Bench warmers" applied to Christians. Let's get out of our seats and go into the streets. It's time for a fresh wind in the Windy City. We must win souls for Christ and have victory for Jesus. But there will be no victory without a battle.

I've learned that's where God wants me . . . in the battle, in the Windy City.

13

If God Is for Us

Toni Armstrong Sample

My father's favorite Bible verse is *"If God is for us, who can be against us?"* Romans 8:31b (NIV). His belief must have been intensely positive that nothing anyone ever did against him could be greater, or stronger, than the love God had for him.

When I think of these words I am comforted by the peace this verse is to me. There are people in this world who do things to hurt others. How wonderful it is to live with the knowledge that God's love is greater than all negative things that could ever be said, or done, about us or to us. When Jesus talked to people who were skeptical, he looked at them and said, *"With man this is impossible, but with God all things are possible"* Matthew 19:26 NIV.

My mother's favorite verse is Romans 8:38 NIV, *"I am convinced that neither death nor life, neither angels nor demons, neither the present nor the future, nor any powers, neither height nor depth, nor anything else in all creation, will be able to separate us from the love of God that is in Christ Jesus our Lord."*

Dad's verse asks a question. Mom's verse is a positive statement.

As I think of these two people I understand how the verses perfectly fit who they are. Dad was an engineer who was always looking at the different angles of things, troubleshooting, figuring out how something worked. Questioning was a part of his career, and the personality with which God blessed him.

Mom takes everything exactly as presented. She is a woman who trusts. When my steady beau and I would go out for an evening with our high school friends, her last words as we exited the front door were, "Have fun kids, and remember, I trust you."

I could not do anything to break that trust. Now that she has reached the age of ninety-seven, I still don't want to break that bond of amazing trust. Because of that strong bond of trust between Mom and me, I feel strongly about the bond of trust between God and me.

Looking at the verses that come between my parent's favorite verses, I noticed what is told by Paul, the author, as he wrote to the church in Rome.

Verses 32–37 NIV read:

He who did not spare his own Son, but gave him up for us all – how will he not also, along with him, graciously give us all things? Who will bring any charge against those whom God has chosen? It is God who justifies. Who then is the one who condemns? No one. Christ Jesus who died – more than that, who was raised to life – is at the right hand of God and is also interceding for us. Who shall separate us from the love of Christ? Shall trouble or hardship or persecution or famine or nakedness or danger or sword? As it is written: "For your sake we face death all day long; we are considered as sheep to be slaughtered." No, in all these things we are more than conquerors through him who loved us.

Many of the questions we have regarding the mystery that surrounds our Creator, have no answer on earth. One most frequently asked is, "Where is heaven?" That's where faith becomes our guide.

Faith in something we cannot see asks the question, "Do you believe?"

God has told us that if we have the faith of a mustard seed, that's all we need. As we read and study his word we will find answers to many of our questions.

One example: If God is for us, who can be against us?

The answer: No one.

14

A Sinking Friendship

Ivette Ellis

Because I was their outsourced financial representative, I was convinced that the hospital would hire me. A contract between my employer and the hospital was pending the hospital's approval.

My friend lived near the hospital so she and I agreed that I could live with her and her family, while things were settled at the hospital.

I moved in and the first part of the month passed by with very few hiccups, until she made a surprising announcement. She was going to turn the large house over to someone else and move into a smaller one. That same day, she started packing and moved later that week.

In the wake of her tornado-like evacuation, she commented, "You can come with us, if you want." The "if you want" suggested to me that I really wasn't welcome. Her nonchalant words hung in the air like a cloud filled with rain getting ready to pour down on me.

I was in a precarious situation. After all, I had relocated from Atlanta. Although completely disenchanted, I had reasoned that the best solution to my predicament, temporary accommodations with my friend, would allow me time to find housing without being rushed into a big decision.

After I heard and felt the resentment behind her "join us if you want," our conversations started to feel like fingernails scraping a chalkboard. Still, I wanted to remain amicable. I felt it would be only a short time before the hospital would call me to come in. Reluctantly, I agreed to join her and her family one week after they moved.

When I went to move in the following Saturday night, the house was already dark, so I turned the doorknob as slowly as possible and entered on my tiptoes, determined not to awaken anyone.

The following morning, my friend asked, "How did you get in?" The strong sarcastic tone in her voice, made my stomach cringe with uneasiness.

"I opened the door and walked in," I replied. She was quick to tell me that she had locked the door prior to going to bed the night before.

My blood pressure shot straight up. "Why would you do that knowing that I was coming over?" I asked. She didn't reply. In fact, I never did get a reply from her.

So, there I stood, essentially homeless and possibly jobless, too. I prayed for divine intervention.

One day, maybe two, had passed when my employer called to tell me the hospital was not ready to accept the terms of the contract. My first reaction was failure, rejection and defeat. But my second reaction flooded me with the truth that I was still employed and could move back to Atlanta — which I did, in a hurry.

Several years later, I ran into my former friend — at a gas station, of all places. We had a brief conversation in which I shared that I was completing my undergraduate degree and planning to pursue my graduate degree. Her facial expression held astonishment.

She tried to dissuade me from completing my education. But that did not work. Then, as if she needed to offset her astonishment, she invited me to a craft event soon to take place near her home. I declined the invitation with all the graciousness I could muster, wished her well, and drove away.

I know I am not the only person to experience such a disastrous event. Still, the stress of trying to relocate, encountering rejection from a friend, and facing possible unemployment, all at the same time, had made me feel like my life was unraveling.

I've thought about what I could have done differently. First, made sure that the hospital had in fact signed the new contract, before I moved. Second, locate housing independent of relying on a friend.

Do all friendships turn out sour? Not at all. The key in this situation is that I dismissed the red flags which indicated this friend was not trustworthy.

In the last fifteen years, I have learned a few valuable lessons. Genuine friends value their relationships, are dependable, do not discourage the other's goals.

Today, I'm grateful that I completed my educational goals. I relish the honest friendships in my life and attribute them to increased self-awareness, embracing the beauty of boundaries, and inviting God's guidance into the development of new acquaintances.

15

Courage and Sacrifice

Lt. Col. Robert B. Robeson

"I think I should say one word, too, a special word, about the Dust Offs — the medevacs. This was a great group of men. All those who flew them, all those who did it. Courage above and beyond the call of duty was sort of routine to them. It was a daily thing, part of the way they lived. That's the great part and it meant so much to every last man who served there. Whether he ever got hurt or not, he *knew Dust Off was there.*"

General Creighton W. Abrams, Jr., Army Chief of Staff
Remarks by the late, Army's Chief of Staff,
General Creighton W. Abrams, Jr.
at the AAAA Honors Luncheon
held at the Sheraton Park Hotel
Washington, D.C. October 13, 1972.

The recollection of that unbelievable medical evacuation mission on Saturday, September 13, 1969 — two days prior to my 27th birthday — flashed through my mind.

I was standing bareheaded at attention under a scorching early afternoon sun in Da Nang, South Vietnam in our unit area on the shore of scenic Da Nang Harbor. It was mid-March 1970. The aide for Col. D.W. Pratt (the U.S. Army 95th Evacuation Hospital commander) was reading my citation for a Distinguished Flying Cross, which our entire Dust Off crew had received.

The memory, alone, of the danger and drama surrounding that mission was enough to make me sweat even more than I already was. I'd been in-country barely two months, but had already seen more of war at age 26 than I had ever cared to imagine. As John

Keats so aptly stated in his poem, "Nothing ever becomes real 'til it is experienced . . . ."

That's part of the reason why Chief Warrant Officer 2 (CW2) John Ball would mean so much to me. John was 32 years of age and had four children. This former U.S. Marine, turned U.S. Army aviator, was an old soldier of many military campaigns around the planet.

As operations officer for the 236th Medical Detachment (Helicopter Ambulance), headquartered at Red Beach, I'd scheduled to spend five days (September 10th-14th) as John's copilot. He was an aircraft commander and also one of our instructor pilots. We'd be stationed at our field site aid station at Landing Zone (LZ) Baldy located approximately 25 miles south of Da Nang. We gathered the rest of our crew — a medic and crew chief — and flew out to cover action that would keep us in the air over 31 hours, which included 12½ night hours, evacuating dead and wounded.

On September 11th, our supported infantry units were hit hard by the North Vietnamese Army (NVA). We were airborne eleven hours that day and ten hours on the 12th. We'd slide out of the sky on mission after mission, picking up torn and broken bodies.

We'd already flown over three hours before the sun came up on the 13th and had finally shut down to snatch a few Zs. About mid-morning, another mission was called in. We quickly scrambled after only a momentary rest. We were in the air, returning from this mission with a load of patients, when a second urgent request was broadcast over our FM radio. It was another insecure LZ reportedly under heavy enemy fire. While I called for UH-1C helicopter gunship support from the Firebirds, who also flew out of Baldy, John landed and unloaded these patients. Then he lifted off again in the direction of four Americans who had been seriously wounded by small arms fire.

Between air-to-air and air-to-ground communications, I said my usual silent prayer for our safety and the safety of our patients.

As we approached the area of contact a few klicks (kilometers) southwest of LZ Center — a towering artillery base jutting nearly straight up hundreds of feet above the surrounding terrain — concentrated artillery fire could be seen bracketing a heavily wooded area. This was soon cut off so our two gunships could make gun runs on enemy positions before we went in. After their second pass, I called for smoke to mark where the ground troops wanted us to land.

Then John bottomed the collective control with his left hand, which governs the pitch of the blades, as we transitioned into a smooth, 4,000 feet per minute descent. As we fell out of the sky, John reminded me to stay close to my controls, something he'd never mentioned before.

John always flew with the force trim on. There was an on/off switch located between us, at the top of the pedestal beneath the instrument panel. With that switch on there was an artificial feel or force applied to the cyclic which held it in one position. You could move the cyclic against this force but if you released pressure the cyclic would return to its last trimmed position. There was an intermittent force trim release button on the cyclic stick grip that if depressed and held, released the force trim. John trimmed the aircraft — through the use of the button on the cyclic stick — so that there was aft pressure on the cyclic at all times. That way the nose of our bird would automatically rise should he be wounded or his hand come off the cyclic stick. When we were barreling along at 140 miles per hour, a few feet above the ground, with people shooting at us, that extra split second of time was important. It could mean the difference between survival or becoming a messy Huey sandwich in a sewage-filled rice paddy or some hover-hole in the jungle.

Personally, I never flew with the force trim on because it caused me to lose my touch on the cyclic when doing many dramatic combat maneuvers. But because John chose to do so, we'd all soon benefit from a special message that would manifest itself directly to my heart.

As we continued a rapid descent and began our approach to the LZ from the west, "Willie-Peter" — white phosphorous rockets — that had been fired ahead of us by our gunships suddenly obscured the red smoke from the grenade the ground troops had thrown out.

John grabbed a bunch of pitch with the collective in his left hand and began a tight, 360-degree, cyclic climb to his left. With the bad guys reported to be so close to the wounded, making the ultimate misjudgment of landing to the wrong area could have been disastrous.

"Tango 2-4, this is Dusty," I broadcast over our FM radio. "We lost your smoke because of the Willie Pete. If you could pop one more, we'll attempt another approach. Over."

"Negative on the smoke, Dusty. We're all out down here."

"Okay, we'll drop our own smoke," John said.

With 2-4 visually guiding us, we barreled in on two runs 10 feet above the LZ tree line as our crew chief dropped smoke grenades under heavy enemy fire. On the second pass, we finally hit our target. Then John circled back to land.

It was because the LZ was so tight, we couldn't turn around to go out the way we'd come in for fear of hitting someone or something with our tail rotor, that John made the decision he did.

"I'm going up and over to get out of here," John said over the intercom.

As we topped the trees that hid the enemy force, at about 75 feet, AK-47 — Soviet assault rifles used by the NVA — and other automatic weapons hosed-us-down from beneath and to both sides of the aircraft.

From that split second of time, for the next minute or so, everything seemed to occur in super-slow motion.

"We're going to crash!" John suddenly yelled into his mike. "My cyclic's been shot away!"

I immediately looked over to see him sweeping his cyclic stick in wide circles around the cockpit . . . movements that should have made the aircraft spin in circles. But our bird didn't respond. As the

Huey's nose began a dive toward the trees, I instinctively reached for my set of controls.

"I've got it," I said.

This is it, I distinctly remember thinking, as enemy rounds continued ventilating our bird. *Today is the day I'm going to die!* Suddenly the shooting ceased. We'd flown out of the enemy's field of fire.

When I grasped my cyclic, it was immediately evident that force trim pressure no longer existed. The switch was on, but it had zero affect. An inner whisper, that I believe came from God, impressed me to be extremely careful and not move my cyclic more than necessary to stay out of the tops of the trees that our skids were now brushing. I gently eased the cyclic toward me and we began a shallow ascent.

At that moment, the red rpm warning light on the instrument panel illuminated, accompanied by gut-wrenching shrieks in our flight helmets from the low-rpm audio warning. In rapid succession, the yellow master caution light at the top of the instrument panel was next to make its appearance. Glancing down at the emergency panel on the pedestal between us, I saw that the Engine Oil light was illuminated.

Dust Off pilots set normal engine rpm for our operations between 6,400-6,600. Ours had bled off to nearly 5,800 in seconds. I knew that if something didn't happen in a hurry, our bird would soon have more characteristics of a crowbar than a crow.

We'd obviously been hit in the engine and oil lines, among other places. Although John had been grazed in his left leg by a round, he immediately reached over to the pedestal and placed the governor switch into the emergency position. This provided enough extra engine power to momentarily remain airborne while we discussed our limited options.

We both realized that our engine was losing a lot of oil and could instantaneously seize. If it did, I'd have to auto-rotate — descending on the energy in the blades, alone, rather than the engine — to make a forced landing. This would mean I'd also have to make a dramatic movement with my cyclic stick at the bottom to flare and dissipate airspeed before touchdown, even if we found an open area. Otherwise, I'd have to make a tree landing.

"What do you want me to do?" I asked John, as I slowly eased in pitch with my left hand, inched up to 500 feet AGL — above ground level — and attained a comfortable 80 knots of indicated airspeed.

"Just keep us in the air," he answered quietly. "Just fly. Maybe we can find a place to put it down where we won't hurt ourselves."

If our engine failed, I wanted to make a running landing. LZ Ross lay straight ahead, six miles northwest of LZ Center and eleven miles southwest of LZ Baldy. Ross was located in relatively flat terrain and had a large open area where we often picked up patients. But this was still four to five minutes away.

"I'm gonna shoot for Ross."

"Okay," John said. "I'll call Da Nang and have them get another bird out there to pick us up."

"Sir," SP5 Bill Bergman — our crew chief — broke in on the intercom, "we got our guns at four o'clock high. Looks like they're following us in."

John alerted the Firebirds to our dilemma and one of them edged close enough under our blades to confirm that we were leaking oil all over the sky.

I did some silent praying en route, too. Having been raised as a preacher's kid gave me a wealth of appreciation and insight for this spiritual involvement. I thanked God for allowing us to reach our four patients and for getting all of us out of that miserable LZ in one piece. Then I asked Him, if it was His will, to help me keep the rest of the pieces intact until we reached LZ Ross.

I bounced our skids a couple of times on the uneven ground at LZ Ross in a short running landing. And when the ground run stopped . . . *so did our Lycoming jet engine.* All 1,300 horses expired at once. Simultaneously, John and I turned to look at each other.

Neither of us said a word. We both realized what had just happened.

We transferred our patients and medic to one of the Firebird gunships and they both lifted off for the aid station at Baldy.

Then John and I did a post-flight inspection. We confirmed that all of the engine oil was gone. The last of it formed two small pools in the red clay beneath the aircraft.

As we both stood in the shadow of our tail boom, John looked at me and said softly, "Someone else was flying with us today." His statement was a surprise because he'd never expressed any type of spiritual viewpoint to me before.

I nodded in agreement. There had never been any doubt of that in my mind.

It was hours later before we knew "the rest of the story," as Paul Harvey would say. After our maintenance crew arrived and sling-loaded — retrieving the aircraft by hoisting it out beneath a large U.S. Marine CH-53 helicopter through the use of a sling — the bird back to Red Beach in Da Nang, one of them took me aside. He told me he'd reached up and merely touched my cyclic stick. It had broken off in his hand.

After removing the metal floor paneling and taking apart the control, he discovered that only a sliver of metal had been holding it in place. That's why I couldn't feel any force trim pressure against my hand. One of the bursts of automatic weapons fire from John's side of the aircraft had completely severed his cyclic stick and had continued its flight beneath our floor panels to nearly take mine with it.

That soft, inner voice had been right on target. To this day, I firmly believe God, or one of His guardian angels, warned me not to move my cyclic any more than necessary and kept our wounded bird flying for over five minutes with little or no oil in the engine.

Simply stated, it was a miracle. This is the only explanation that suffices for what happened so long ago.

I'm now 74 years of age, but I often reflect on that mission and my 986 other medevac missions in one year for 2,533 patients from both sides of the action. What I discovered — after having seven helicopters shot up by enemy fire and being shot down twice — was that in that kind of rescue work you never knew whose life you would step into or who would step into yours. But, as I discovered over and over in my 19-year flying career, God was always in control of my life regardless of the situation. My faith in Him kept me going and gave me the strength to do more than I ever thought I was capable of doing.

Postscript

I flew with John Ball for three more years at the 63rd Medical Detachment (Helicopter Ambulance) in Landstuhl, West Germany. He retired from the military after 20 years of service in 1974 and continued his aviation career in civilian life.

While logging with a helicopter in the Bitterroot National Forest near Medicine Hot Springs in Montana on April 19, 1979, a mechanical malfunction occurred that caused his aircraft to invert and crash. He died that day, at age 42, along with Thomas Hewitt, his 32-year-old copilot. Ironically, Hewitt was also from La Grande, Oregon, where I graduated from high school.

I flew from Lincoln, Nebraska to his home in Portland, Oregon for the funeral on April 25, 1979. After all of the times he had "carried" me in combat and in Europe, I was honored to be asked to help carry him to his final resting place on a magnificent mountainside in a picturesque area of Portland he loved.

Sometimes people come into our lives and leave giant footprints on our hearts and souls. That's what John did with me. I will never forget him or our special friendship, both in and out of the cockpit, and on three continents.

16

Going Home

Diana C. Derringer

Return home and tell how much God has done for you.

Luke 8:39 NIV

As soon as we entered the driveway, his questions began. "Who lives here?"

"We do," I said.

"How long have you lived here?"

"We live here together. Remember, I'm your wife." He then stared until recognition crossed his face.

"When can we go home?"

"We are home. This is where we live now."

Over and over I gently prodded his memory.

Following a heart attack, stroke, fall resulting in severe brain injury, and lack of oxygen when his heart and lungs stopped functioning on December 10, 2009, medical staff did not believe my husband would survive. Miraculously he did. Then they anticipated the need for long-term care.

Yet he walked into our home in less than four weeks, a home he failed to recognize. After several days, he began recalling the move to our house, and his questions changed.

"When did we leave the old house?"

"About nine years ago."

"When are the other people leaving?"

"We're the only ones here now. Two former university students visited a few days before your fall. But they're gone now."

"Where do we keep the soap?" Or shampoo, bowls, or countless other items used daily. We found them together.

One part of our routine he never questioned was our evening time of Bible reading and prayer. After I finished reading a Bible passage each night, he would clasp my hand in his before we prayed and turned out the lights. That had been our pattern for years.

His need for outpatient therapy lasted only a few weeks. He quickly progressed from walker to cane to unassisted, but supervised. We continued a series of balance exercises at home for a few weeks. Gradually he regained full independence and now seldom needs a cane.

Bit by bit his memory also returned. He went from little long-term and almost no short-term memory to primarily short-term memory loss. Those who know us well marvel at God's mighty work in my husband's life and the witness this experience has provided. We continue to pray that his story, both verbal and written, will point everyone we meet to the Great Physician. We want them to know that, whether we experience God's miraculous physical healing or not, God offers spiritual healing to all.

The summer following my husband's hospitalizations we took a short vacation. Although a refreshing change, it also proved exhausting for us. As we returned, the closer we came to Kentucky the more excited we grew. Finally, we crossed the state line, and with joy my heart echoed his spoken sentiment, "I'll certainly be glad when we get home."

Yet, that experience pales in comparison to our rejoicing when we one day cross the threshold of our eternal home.

17
Daddy's Girl

Margaret Peterson

When our hoped-for baby girl was born, she was a boy! Murray and I each held a tiny hand and fell in love with him. Thoughts of a daughter fled from our minds.

But our pleasure in Bruce in time, recreated the longing for a girl. No second child arrived after one year, two years, three. We sought medical help without success. There were doctors' appointments, too, for Murray's declining health. Neither problem had a solution.

Murray became the stay at home parent and I found employment. We adjusted to our new routine but I still longed for a daughter to complete our family. I asked the Lord for another baby but my hopes faded by the time Bruce turned nine. I accepted life with Murray at home, Bruce at school and myself at work.

A year later, to my happy amazement, I discovered that God had, in His own time, answered my prayers. We were having another baby.

My gift to Murray on our wedding anniversary would be to share this blessing with him. I thought he might guess my news by my jubilant actions and constant smile. "Darling," I said and reached the restaurant table for his hands, "we're having a baby."

Disbelief settled on his face. It turned ashen. His stricken look smashed my exhilaration to fragments. "No! Elizabeth. No. Not another baby." He choked. "Say it isn't true." When I nodded, he closed his eyes and shook his head. "I can't work. How can we bring up another child?"

"But . . ." I could hardly speak. "This baby could be the daughter we always wanted." My words were futile. Our evening was ruined and we drove home in silence.

The next morning Murray said, "Having another baby is irresponsible. We're barely able to live on your wages now. We can't do it. I want you to have an abortion."

Get rid of this child that God was sending us? My mind reeled; my heart pounded. I ran from the room and slammed the door to shut out Murray's words, "I want you to phone Dr— "

Murray brought up the subject again and again. I remained steadfast in my conviction to protect and keep this child. One night, at the end of another argument, Murray threw a book against the wall, saying, "I'm a lousy father! I can't provide for my son and now you want to bring another child into the world." He ran a hand over his face. "You're asking too much of me, Elizabeth. You've got to have an abortion or I'll leave."

Having difficulty breathing, I struggled to get out the words. "No matter what you threaten, I accept this baby from God. He will provide for us." I would trust Him. My breath returned as peace enveloped me.

Murray did not leave. But I sensed his emotional abandonment.

The stress of the coming child caused a further decline in his health and depression clouded over him. In contrast, I rejoiced at the new life within me and held tightly to God's hand for the support I needed.

I arranged for time off from work and prepared a layette. By faith, I polished the baby bracelet and locket that had been mine, and my mother's before me. I pictured the doctor saying, "It's a girl."

In my mind I heard my response, "Thank You, Lord." After nine years of waiting I trusted He would give me my heart's desire.

And He did. Our daughter, Grace, was a lovely infant, the pride of her big brother and the joy of my life. To my delight she soon became, for Murray, a Daddy's Girl. Her first smile was for him and when she learned to crawl, it was in his direction.

Her first steps were toward him and as she faltered at his feet, Murray grabbed her up and set her on his knee. "Sweetheart, you are precious," he whispered and hugged her to him.

"She is, isn't she?" I said.

Murray looked at me and nodded. I saw tears shimmer in his blue eyes. "Elizabeth, you were right." His voice was hoarse as he added, "If I'd had my way we would have missed out on all the happiness our baby girl has brought us."

He put his daughter gently down on the carpet and came to embrace me. "Grace is God's gift to us. You chose her name well because it is reminder to me of God's grace to me."

Recently the four of us celebrated Grace's tenth birthday. I looked around the decorated table at my family and praised God for His gifts of life and love, prayed for, waited for, and accepted by all of us, with thanksgiving.

18

Journey into Exclusivity

Sherry Boykin

Your Creator will be your husband. The Lord Almighty is his name"
Isaiah 54:5 NLT

There it was, plain as day.

A verse so steeped in nuptial goodness I could hardly read it without a swatch of tulle hanging from my head — the verse that encouraged me to have an impromptu wedding ceremony as I flew to the Peruvian Amazon for the first time.

I was a new missionary, still somewhat disappointed that I wasn't beginning that new chapter with a husband. Then I realized that wasn't true! I *was* beginning that journey with a husband, and not just in an allegorical sense.

I was dead serious.

With a ring I bought from a gift shop in Panama during my layover, my Bible, and my vows, I declared myself the bride of Christ so definitively that I knew any earthly mate God might one day give would have to understand he was my second husband, and that the first one wasn't going away.

I was a happy wife, until somewhere along the way the fact of *my* husband being *your* husband, and *her* husband, and the husband of all who read Isaiah 54:5, became a little unsettling.

And pardon the revisiting of my New York City roots, but didn't that make God a two-timer? And a two-timer a zillion times over?

I wanted exclusivity.

And yes, though I knew God was big enough to handle me and anyone else in the universe, there was something bittersweet and polygamous about having to share my intimate partner with every Tallulah, Jane, and Ally.

Then God settled my angst.

One weekend on a twenty-six-hour ride on a public Amazon River launch I curled up in my hammock, decidedly ignoring the stench, gawks and squeals of animals around me, and the swing-swish-foot-brushing of people below me, took out my Bible, and got down to doing business with God.

I was good and ready — not exactly mad, but fully-armed with what I knew were formidable inquiries as to what in the world God was doing in my life.

My coworkers, a Peruvian couple from Lima, had travelled back to the capital for medical treatments. It looked as though the wife may have had breast cancer, and there was no available treatment for that in the jungle where we were.

I was afraid of losing a great friend, and their weeks-long trip left me to do our church-planting work alone in our village for an extended period. And it seemed that much of what I did at that time became increasingly isolating. For short stays someone might travel with me or come upriver to help with a particular program or something, but they'd all eventually go back to what they previously did.

And so on that particular day, on the heaviest day of my cycle, after getting neck to toe and backpack soaked falling into the river while boarding a launch to go twenty-six hours without a bathroom I could fit into, preparing to speak at a retreat at the end of those twenty-six hours, and as lonely as lonely could be, I felt a little bit picked on.

And so I gave it to the Lord . . . all in one breath . . . .

*Lord, aren't I okay with you? I love you, I serve you every day, and I even drink masato (*a thick drink made from cooked yucca that is chewed, spit out, and fermented) *'til it gets stuck in my teeth. Why, then can't I have what I really want? Why can't I have what I have been asking for? Why can't I have a permanent ministry partner?*

Just then, at the ceremonial ringing of the launch's dinner bell — just before the swing-swish-foot-brushing turned into a wild run for arroz con frijoles (rice with beans), the Lord spoke to my heart so clearly that He may as well have said it out loud: *Why would I give you away to someone else when I don't fully have you myself?*

I never once wondered if I understood Him correctly, never once imagined what smart-alecky response I might offer to the One who knew me better than I knew myself.

He wanted me to know that in all my missionary-ing I had forgotten Him, my husband — the One to whom I was betrothed as I flew to the Peruvian Amazon. While busy with the teaching and discipling associated with missionary work, I neglected my personal relationship with the Lord.

And He missed me. My husband, the King of the universe, my Savior, missed me and wanted me to be fully-connected to Him before ever extending my hand to anyone else in marriage.

Suddenly, I didn't care about Tallulah, Jane, or Ally, because I knew no other soul in the universe had *my* particular relationship.

I had my exclusivity — my marriage with my Savior.

19

But . . . the *Titanic* Sank

Alice Klies

When I became an empty nester, I yearned to find a new purpose for my life. Most moms, faced with the plight of their children going off to college, are in their forties or early fifties. I had just turned sixty-five. I needed one of those "Aha!" moments. You know, one with the music of the smooth-sailing *Titanic* ringing in my ears.

One Sunday, our youth pastor at church approached me. "Did you ever think about volunteering with the youth department? I could sure use someone to help with the high school group."

"Really?" I questioned. "Don't you have a bunch of parents willing to help?"

"Not really, and I'd love to have a few mature volunteers who can do some mentoring. Think about it."

I went home and proceeded to convince my husband that this was something we should do together. "Just think sweetheart," I said. "We could do this together. It might keep us young."

He peeked over the top of his glasses, giving me one of those, "You've got to be kidding," looks.

But I knew I'd win.

So, together we me met with the Sunday school group on Sunday mornings, and then attended the youth events on Sunday nights, a time filled with silly games, raucous music, fellowship and Bible study.

Little did I know how much this generation gap, this look into the life of teens today through volunteering, would change me. When I took on the challenge of mentoring and coming alongside teenagers, I never expected I'd learn something from them.

My heart ached when I witnessed the looks on faces of kids

from dysfunctional families who were verbally abused or neglected. I didn't expect that I'd feel joy and excitement while I watched teens, not related to me, walk across a graduation stage. I didn't believe I could stay up on New Year's Eve night until two o'clock the next morning, rejoicing to teenage exuberance.

I stood alongside teens who learned to care about the homeless, the needy, the blind and I realized they willingly took part in making a difference in someone else's life. I walked beside teens that walked or jogged for a cancer cure or a right to life event. I learned that the news media only tells us stories about the bad things in which teens are sometimes involved.

When our youth pastor asked if I'd like to be a leader at the annual summer camp trip, I jumped at the chance. By this time, I felt fully accepted as the oldest youth leader.

As I started to pack my blood pressure medicine, Tylenol and extra-long Bermuda shorts, I laughed out loud and questioned if I'd lost my mind to take this weeklong trip to the mountains with fifty teenagers.

I reached down to massage my aching hip as I took the first step into the bus, already filled with shouting, over-zealous teens.

One of the boys put his hand out. "Here, Mrs. K, let me help you. I saved a seat for you in the front. It'll be easier for you to get out at potty breaks."

I didn't know whether I wanted to hit him or hug him. His big smile softened my heart. I just said, "Thank you."

I settled into the seat, looked around and sighed. Every student held an iPhone, iTouch, iPad or Tablet. They frantically typed away. I glanced down at my bag. My tattered crossword puzzle book peeked out from a zipper side pocket. *Did I remember to bring my pencil sharpener?* I mused, and then snickered.

Ten hours later, we arrived at our destination. I gasped for breath as I trudged up a long hill to the girls' dorm. *Must be the altitude,* I guessed.

I hoped I was prepared for the drama that almost always plagues teen girls away at camp. I soothed tears, I prayed for and with girls about hopes, dreams, fears and choices. I became the listening ear, an arm around a shoulder and a cheerleader when they needed it.

The next morning, after worship, the youth had free time and they eagerly signed up for the zip line over a deep canyon. I had no idea that roles were about to reverse; that I was going to need the listening ear, the arm around a shoulder and a battery of cheerleaders.

I watched from the corner of my eyes as one by one our teens ascended a mountainside to zip-line across a canyon. I didn't share with them that I was terrified of heights. I couldn't even climb a ladder. Three steps up and I might lose a meal. One of the camp leaders geared the last teen up for a zip and announced, "Any of you leaders who want to zip can gear up after the last teen goes."

Tim ran up to me.

"Come on Mrs. K. It's your turn."

"No . . . no thanks Tim. Not really my cup of tea. I don't exactly like heights."

"Aw . . . come on Mrs. K. You can do this. Anything is possible with God." Then he laughed.

"Don't pull that God-thing on me Tim. I'm sure God doesn't want me to do this."

Julie, another leader, put her arm around my shoulder. "I'll go with you. They zip two at a time. I'll be right there with you, right along with God."

Somehow I found myself geared up and starting the ascent to the tower. Even with encouragement, I needed to stop many times to catch my breath from the steep climb. The sting of tears threatened to fall and give way to my fear.

A thirty-foot ladder loomed in front of me. Four steps up, my legs wobbled. Ten more steps and bile collected in the back of my throat. Voices from above chanted. "You're almost here. Look up and we will help you."

Three young men stood at the top of the ladder with outstretched hands.

Once at the top, I said. "I can't open my eyes. I can't do this."

By this time Julie stood behind me. She whispered in my ear. "Just you, God, and me. We're doing this."

The clip snapped onto the zip-line and Julie hollered. "On three . . . here we go."

I have absolutely no idea what happened next, except I flew through the air. Julie yelled, "Look at you, Alice. You are flying. You're doing it, girl."

Flying! Like Jack and Rose on the *Titantic*. How enthralling!

But . . . the *Titanic* sank. Jack . . . didn't survive.

After I quit screaming, a peace settled over me.

I opened my eyes and took in the majesty of God's creation. Yes, I calmly thought. I did it. I began to sob.

As I dangled above the world and waited to be helped down on yet another tall ladder, I looked below at a throng of teens that I had mentored and cared for. Now they were doing the same for me. I had volunteered to be a light in the lives of a teen youth group and here they stood clapping and cheering for me.

I think I got the best deal out of the relationships and volunteering brought on new meaning for this old gal. Yes, Rose . . . and Alice . . . survived!

Mostly, I enjoyed the resounding *Titanic* music I heard during this amazing "Aha!" moment.

20

Anger's Threat

Bennie McDonald
as told to Nanette Thorsen-Snipes

On a cold day in March, 1997, my wife and I headed for Monterey, Kentucky, after the Kentucky River spilled out of its banks. We stopped at a service station at Interstate 75 in Georgia.

As I pumped gas, a woman approached me, glanced at our relief uniforms and asked, "Where are you people going?"

"A small town in Kentucky to help with the floods," I said. I watched compassion grow in her eyes as she pressed sixty dollars into my palm.

"Take this to them," she whispered, then walked away.

I tucked the money into my jacket pocket, thanking God for generous people. I knew someone could use that money.

We drove all day and by nighttime, the rain began pounding the car. It slashed across our windshield in sheets. At times, we couldn't even see the car in front of us. Once in Monterey, our headlights lit up mud-covered streets. On both sides of the narrow streets, stood junked TVs, sofas, and other debris contaminated by the mud. And the smell — once the stench reaches the nose, it stays.

I quickly learned that a flood is different from other natural disasters. Floods leave debris permeated with bacteria, which must be decontaminated. Houses, in many cases, have to be ripped apart and washed down with a bleach mixture before they're fit to live in.

The rain stopped the next day, but the temperature dropped. Raindrops froze on the hood of my car. When our Communications Unit set up that morning, I had trouble breathing. I was sure the problem was due to the bitter cold. Ignoring my symptoms, I threw myself into my work.

As a ham radio operator with an Amateur Extra rating, I provided timely information about supplies, personnel in the area, equipment and special assistance. I helped coordinate the units, keeping the operation running smoothly.

Later that day, I saw Barbara Jarvis and her young son ripping out a floor in their house. I watched them work well into the night. When her husband got off his job, the two of them labored until the whole family collapsed into one bed — the only one they'd salvaged.

The morning of our second day, some of us from the Unit offered to help the Jarvis family. I slogged through mud and began tearing down sheetrock. As I worked, I felt as if a vice gripped my lungs. I couldn't breathe in that house. It seemed as if the dampness just about shut my lungs down. I shrugged it off, thinking I had a touch of the flu.

Ripping out a piece of wet sheetrock, I remembered the last time I worked that hard on a house. It was just before my wife had died of cancer in 1986. Although she was sick, Ann had wanted to build a log home. It took me six months to build the home while holding down a job at the post office. I also took care of my wife and became physically and emotionally spent.

Ann died a month after we moved in. I was angry with God for putting me through so much anguish. I couldn't foresee that three years later God would put me through another trial.

In 1989, my thirty-year-old daughter died at the hands of her husband. When I got to the mobile home the day she died, I was so enraged I slammed my fist into the side of the structure. That debilitating anger stayed with me for a long time. *Why is this happening to me?* I asked God. Every day, I felt I was walking through fire.

Then in 1996, my present wife and I began volunteering for the Georgia Baptist Disaster Relief — an organization offering the love of God into communities hit by disasters. By this time, I had come to grips with my anger. I felt it was time to help others. So when the flood hit Monterey, Kentucky, I was ready.

Being able to help the Jarvis family tear down the sheetrock and pressure-wash some of the floors with disinfectant, gave me deep satisfaction. I was really helping someone who needed it. But every breath I took became an effort.

After finishing the job and returning to Georgia, my symptoms worsened. On May 1, I went home sick from my postal job.

About mid-June, I finally told my boss that standing all day at the postal window was unbearable. That day inside his office, I lifted my pants legs. My legs were swollen from my knees to my feet. The skin was so taut it looked as if it would pop if anyone touched me. Breathing was even more difficult.

As I faced my boss that day, I'm sure he could see my fear. "I'm scared to death," I said. "I don't know what's wrong with me."

My boss shook his head in disbelief. "You've got to see a doctor, Bennie."

I left work that day and did just that, and for the next few days, I endured a battery of tests including cat scans, X-rays, and biopsies.

On June 14, I was scheduled for exploratory surgery. In my hospital bed I winced, remembering the night before when the doctor had removed more than two liters of fluid from my chest cavity. But that morning, what I'd feared most became reality — the earlier biopsies indicated lung cancer. I knew the gravity of my situation and, choking back tears, I gave the doctor permission to remove anything ominous.

Lying in bed, I thought, *This isn't fair, Lord. I've lost Ann to cancer, and my daughter was murdered. I've tried to do what you want. I've helped others. What do you want from me?*

A young nurse stepped into my room, interrupting my thoughts. "The doctor is running late for your exploratory," she said as she checked my IV's.

When she left, I closed my eyes, thankful for a few more moments to myself. Briefly, I recalled Barbara Jarvis' situation in Monterey. When the flood hit, she was out of work most of the week. The unit director and I passed around a disaster relief hat. All of us in the unit put in some money. Remembering the sixty dollars the woman at the gas station gave me, I reached into my pocket and dropped the bills into the hat. *Thank You, Lord, for angels of mercy.*

When we handed Barbara the money, her eyes bristled with tears. "That's exactly what we needed to pay our motel bill," she said. Like many others in Monterey, she asked, "Why are you doing this?"

"Because we want to share God's love," I said.

It was hard to believe how thankful she was for what we'd given her. It was a drop in the proverbial bucket, knowing how her lifestyle had been changed.

Looking at the IV's, my thoughts returned to my own battle. *Have you forgotten me, God?*

Before I left for surgery, I knew there were things I needed to get straight with God. Like Barbara had bravely faced the aftermath of a flood and doing the hard work, I had to do the same. I needed to face the possibility of dying.

It was the hardest thing I'd ever done — facing my own mortality. I took a deep breath, closed my eyes and prayed, "Lord, if I have cancer and I'm going to die, then I accept it. It's now in your hands." Then and there, I made my peace with God. For the first time, I released everything to him — including my anger at the loss of Ann and my daughter.

While being wheeled into surgery, it seemed as though the flames that had consumed me for so long were finally being tamped out. I had a sweet, fragrant peace inside. I went into surgery knowing I was safe in the steady hands of God — no matter what the outcome.

That day, the doctors successfully removed the tumor that had threatened my life. They seemed surprised that the growth was a benign soft-ball-sized tumor attached to the lower lobe of my right lung. Unlike the doctors, I wasn't surprised at all, because I'd released everything to God.

And then I thanked Him for teaching me to let go of anger, and let Him provide peace.

21

Do You Want an Orange, Or . . .?

Margaret Peterson

I stopped in after work to see how Shelly, my friend who was sick with a cold, was doing and give her a bag of oranges. I told her I had time for a short visit before I went to my Bible study group. That prompted our discussion in which she said she believed in God.

I said, "Believing in God doesn't make one a Christian."

She huffed. "Really, Marnie, I don't have a Bible, but I think you're way off on that."

"Let me try again," I said. We were in her elegantly decorated living room and Shelley stretched out on a black leather recliner as I faced her while sitting in a comfortable chair upholstered in silver brocade. "What I meant was that believing in God doesn't make one a Christian. The Bible says the demons believe and tremble."

She stared at me with skeptical green eyes framed by long lashes and mumbled, "Really?" She pulled an afghan over her velvet robe.

"Let me read it to you." I shuffled through the contents of the purse at my feet and pulled out the pocket sized New Testament. I found James 2:19 and read the words I had quoted.

Her eyes narrowed. "So then—" A coughing fit interrupted her and I went to the kitchen for a fresh glass of water.

She drank half the water and reached for a tissue from a box on a nearby glass-topped table. "So then, what is a Christian?"

"Christians are people who believe that Jesus is God's Son who came to die on a cross so their sins can be forgiven. They also believe when he rose from the dead he showed God's power and that they can live an abundant life through this power until they die. Then they can go to heaven to be with him there."

Shelley's eyes never left mine. The room was silent except for the ticking of the ornate clock that hung above the fireplace. I waited for her response.

"You . . . you actually believe this?"

"I do."

"God doesn't accept anyone else into heaven but Christians?"

"Acts 4:12 says there is no other Name given among men by which we must be saved."

"Bu—." A cough caught her next words and mangled them. She swallowed the remaining water and her finger traced the wet circle the glass had left on the table. She put the glass down and glanced at me, then looked down. She rearranged the afghan.

I picked up the Bible and flipped to John 14:6. "Here is what Jesus says." I handed the book to her and put my finger below the verse. I had to strain to hear the words Shelley read.

"*I am the Way, the Truth and the Life. No one comes to the Father except through Me.*" She returned the Bible. "Why is he the only way?"

I smiled. "You and your analytical mind. You should have been a detective instead of a C.E.O." I got up and smoothed my skirt. "I'll get an orange for you while I think about that." I picked up her glass and headed back to the kitchen. Over my shoulder I said, "But you wouldn't earn as high a salary as a private eye." We both laughed.

In the kitchen, flanked by stainless steel appliances, I peeled an orange and prayed for wisdom to answer Shelley's question. I arranged the fruit on a china plate and took a linen napkin from a drawer. I knew my way around her kitchen as she and I had been friends for years. Rarely, though, had this topic come up and I wanted to make the most of the opportunity to tell her of God's love for her as well as his absolute holiness.

I turned on the tap and as water bubbled into her glass I noticed a new photo of Shelley and her son, Len, above the sink. There it was. I thanked the Lord for the idea He had just given me. I strode purposefully back into the living room.

"How's Len liking his new apartment?"

"Len?"

"Yeah." I chuckled at catching her off guard. "You know, your son?"

She grimaced. "Okay, okay. I know who you mean. I was just expecting you to give me an answer and now you've switched subjects."

"Nope. Not at all." I put the plate, glass and napkin on the table.

"Thanks."

I sat across from her. "Len is the example I want to use for an explanation of how I see God's requirements."

She leaned forward. "Go on."

"Okay. This is about two women and the son of one of them. By the way, that's a great photo of you and Len in the kitchen."

Shelley waved her other hand. "Umm. But continue."

Pleased that I had her interest, I said, "Let's say you're one of the women and I'm the other one and I'm not . . ." I paused to search for the right word. "Not, uh, a woman of integrity. And one day I'm in desperate need of money to pay off some gambling debts. I think immediately of my wealthy friend."

She snickered and I held up my hand. "Okay, my financially comfortable friend." We both giggled. "I go to her house several times but she won't answer my knock and yet I see her eye at the security peephole. I know she cares about me but is avoiding me. Then it dawns on me. She found out about my using her name to borrow money that I didn't pay back. She had to cover for me. I knew I wouldn't be getting into her house again."

Shelley's eyebrows went up. I hastened to add, "This isn't a perfect analogy." She grinned.

"I stew about my predicament. How do I get back into her good graces again? Then I hear that her son is coming into town the next day and will visit his mom about noon. I've never met the guy but I wonder if he can be of help to me. I wait at the end of her driveway the following day and when his car turns into it I wave him down. He opens his car window and I tell him I'm a friend of his mom's but I have behaved badly and I'm sorry. I explain how urgently I need his mom's financial assistance.

I can see the sympathy in his eyes. 'I'll talk to Mom and I can make it happen for you.' He leans over and opens the passenger door for me to get in. When we arrive at the house he saunters up to the entrance while I hang back and chew my nails.

He knocks and at once the door opens. His mom hugs her son and then draws back when she sees me behind him. 'Mom, I've brought your friend who is sorry for what she's done. I told her you'd forgive her and forget the past because I'm asking on her behalf.'

My friend looks at her son for a long moment. Then at me. I hold my breath.

'Welcome,' she says and smiles. She swings the door open wide so we both can enter. Not only was my relationship with my friend restored and she lent me money but her son and I became close friends as well."

I leaned back in my chair and watched Shelley process the story. A coughing fit broke her reverie and she reached for the water glass. I said, "It's the same with God. He is holy and we can't be in his presence without being perfect. Since that is impossible for us he sent Jesus, his sinless Son, to act as our representative and bring us to God."

The clock chimed and I glanced at my watch. "Oh, gottta run. I'll stop in tomorrow. Need me to get you anything?"

"Yes." Her green eyes sparkled like emeralds. "A Bible, please."

22

Closing the Door

Norma C. Mezoe

Fired!

The thing I had feared for so long had happened. I hurriedly emptied my desk drawers of personal items as my supervisor glared at me. I worked as though in a dream but the dream was in reality, a living nightmare.

"How could this be happening to me?" I questioned silently. "I've worked so hard and tried to be the best secretary possible and this is my reward?"

My thoughts were flooded with widely ranging emotions as I said goodbye to some of the volunteers in the office. Grasping my possessions, I walked out of the office for the last time.

What would I do now? I was a fifty-one year old former homemaker with a high school education. Who would hire someone with my background? A person who had held only one job in her adult life and now had been fired from even that position. But within the midst of the turmoil, God was touching me with his peace.

Years before my life had been going smoothly when, without warning, my husband of twenty-seven years left me for a younger woman. I stood by helplessly as my husband filed for divorce. Now came a new beginning and a drastic change in my life.

Although I had not been employed outside my home, God opened doors that led to my being hired as the secretary for a nonprofit organization. I praised him for his faithfulness.

At the time of my hiring, the office lacked a supervisor. Since it was a two-employee office, I was basically on my own for several weeks until a supervisor could be hired. Day by day, I prayed my way through frustrations and problems. "Help Lord! I don't know what to do." And he was always there for me. It didn't seem possible that I was doing this work. Alone, I would have sunk, but with God, I walked on waters of faith.

Then Nancy was hired and things began changing. Soon it became evident that Nancy was more interested in redecorating the office than in learning the many facets of managing a busy office. Her work began to suffer and she blamed me for the problems.

It didn't make sense. In the six years I had been employed there, three supervisors had come and gone. I worked well with them, and each gave me good yearly evaluations and pay increases. Why did Nancy dislike me? What would I do if I was fired?

Eventually the day arrived for my yearly evaluation. Because of the hostile atmosphere, Nancy's boss sat in on the meeting. What should have taken only a short time became hours of extreme tension as Nancy twisted the truth about me and my work. When we finally stopped for a break, Nancy and her supervisor left for lunch together.

After lunch, we continued with the evaluation which ended with Nancy giving me a very low rating. This meant I would not receive a needed pay increase and also I would be placed on probation. Tears were threatening to spill over during those hours of stress but I did not allow their release until my long drive home. Then the floodgates opened.

Each day it became harder to go to work. I never knew what Nancy's mood would be. It seemed I could do nothing to please her. Many days she wore a constant scowl and loudly slammed doors to let me know she wasn't happy to be working with me.

Then came the fatal day. I entered my office that morning, not dreaming it would be my last day there. After loading my desk with work that she wanted completed by noon, Nancy left. A few hours later she returned, followed by her boss. The two of them entered Nancy's office, closing the door behind them.

Later, I was called in and asked to sit as Nancy told more lies about my work. I tried to defend myself, but it was useless. The decision had already been made. Nancy handed me a form to sign, stating that I was being dismissed.

She had destroyed my job but she couldn't destroy my faith in a living, loving God. And she couldn't destroy my pride in my work. I walked out of the office, my head held high. God was filling me with his peace in this latest storm in my life.

Unlike the *Titanic*, I didn't sink.

God walked with me as I searched for employment. I felt his peaceful presence as he protected me from the waters of despair.

After being unemployed for only three weeks, I found another job. I had many adjustments to make because the position and working conditions were so different from my first position. Each morning I asked God's help in making the necessary adjustments and I felt his guidance through each day.

I still do not know why I was fired. I do know that a friend of Nancy's was hired to replace me. God had opened the door to my employment and for reasons known only to him, he later allowed the door to be closed to me. In his own way, God was working his plan for my life. I can trust his leading as he continues to do so.

Jeremiah 29:11-12 assures us: *"I know the plans I have for you," declares the Lord, "plans to prosper you and not to harm you, plans to give you hope and a future. Then you will call upon me and come and pray to me, and I will listen to you."* (NIV)

23

Not What I Had in Mind

Stacy Mink

On a cool, crisp Sunday afternoon, I drove from dropping off one child at a lesson to pick up my other child from her practice. As I made my way down the narrow country road I noticed a small lifeless dog ahead in the center of the roadway.

I slowed, and looked out my window at a Boston Terrier that had obviously been hit by another car. I noticed a collar and knew that I not only had to move the poor thing out of the road but if there were a name tag on the collar, I could call the owner. I pulled my van up ahead and parked on the dirt road about 20 yards from where the dog lay.

As I walked toward the dog, a nice car, that appeared to be new, approached and slowed. About the same time I arrived directly in front of the dog, the car had come to a complete stop. The door on the driver's side opened and a woman stepped out of the car. She went into hysterics, screaming, "Roxy? No, no, no! Roxy!"

My heart initially sank over the sorrow this woman displayed, but very quickly its beating accelerated in panic and fear. Was she going to blame me for the death of her beloved pet? Would she curse me, not knowing that I was being a considerate bystander and going out of my way to help?

I watched the lady proceed to scream and cry out in horror and disbelief. I stood frozen in shock for a few seconds before I was able to shake the doubts and fears that initially flooded me.

"Ma'am, I am so sorry about your dog." I said as I gently approached her. "I promise I didn't hit the dog. I stopped to move her and see if she had a name tag on her collar."

The woman continued to scream. "No, no, no, my baby, not my Roxy, why, why, why . . .?" I simply stood beside her with my hand on her shoulder as she knelt, stroking her furry loved one.

After a few minutes I asked her if she had a bag or blanket to put Roxy in, for it would be necessary to wrap her in something due to the blood that was still freshly pooling around her. The lady explained, in between sobs, that she didn't have anything and questioned how could she put Roxy in her brand new car like this? I informed her that I had a plastic poncho and a large reusable shopping bag in the van and I ran to retrieve the items.

When I returned, the woman was still very emotional. She stood back and watched as I wrapped the dog. As I tried to lift and maneuver the limp body into the poncho, my hands became covered in Roxy's blood. While I was still feeling a sense of compassion and willingness to help, my mind began wrestling with frustration toward this woman who just stood there and watched as I did all the dirty work of removing her dead dog from the pavement. Shouldn't she at least be trying to help to some degree instead of just standing there, still an emotional wreck?

I also began feeling frustrated toward God. I was trying to do a good deed and simply move the dog out of the road so why did He allow me to get in this crazy situation, now dealing with blood-saturated hands?

Almost as quickly as the frustration began to rise, I pushed it aside and completed the task of getting Roxy placed in the bag. I handed the bag to the woman and she struggled to the rear of her car. Before opening the trunk, she dropped to her knees again, sobbing over the bag.

I knelt beside her and asked if it would be okay for me to pray. She vigorously nodded and choked out, "Yes."

I prayed for peace and that the joy of her memories with Roxy would sustain her in the times ahead. I thanked the Lord for the love Roxy brought into her life and that she would soon find new blessings and joy to help fill the void of losing Roxy. I thanked God for my presence and being able to help during that difficult time.

As I prayed, I noticed that her sobbing and trembling had

stopped and I could sense the calming that the woman was experiencing. After a few moments of prayer and upon our amen, the lady stood and placed Roxy in the trunk of her car.

As she turned to me, I quickly reminded her of what I had already said, "Ma'am, I promise I didn't hit her." She looked at me with deep appreciation and said ,"I know, I believe you." She proceeded to explain that she was four-months pregnant and her emotions were haywire lately which must be why she was unable to compose herself earlier. She said that she couldn't imagine what she would have done if I weren't there to help. She then hugged me tightly and thanked me sincerely before stepping into her car and driving away.

As I got back into my van and hesitantly placed my hands (with the traces of dried blood) upon the steering wheel, I spoke out loud to God asking Him, "Are you kidding me Lord? I stopped to move the dog and call the owner and You decide to just send her right to me? What just happened is not what I had in mind."

Then, almost as loudly and clearly as I heard my own voice echo through the van, I heard the Lord's voice say in return, "Are my ways not better than yours? I had you right where I needed you and you did just as I was hoping you would."

I burst into tears, realizing that I had both doubted God and yet obeyed Him at the same time. I released tears of sadness for the loss of Roxy as I also cried tears of appreciation for God choosing me to be His hands and feet during the stranger's time of need. As I continued on my way to pick up my child, I had an overwhelming humility and joy for how God had used me in a small but mighty way that day.

It is indeed true that His plans are always better than mine, even when things don't turn out as I anticipate or hope for. I am so grateful for His trust in using me to fulfill His plans even when I doubt them.

24

I Nearly Died

Nanette Thorsen-Snipes

In 1976, I nearly died.

My former husband, Aaron (name changed), held me hostage in our bedroom for hours. He took a gun down from our walk-in closet, closed his hand around the large handgun and grasped a box of bullets. His gray eyes were glazed from drinking, and holding the black gun in his hand, he slowly inserted bullets into each chamber. As each one clicked, I pondered the outcome of my life. I recall praying and asking God to allow me to please see my two little boys grow up.

God mercifully answered my prayer. Years later, in 1983, right after Thanksgiving, my new husband, Jim, and I went grocery shopping. By then, we had four kids, and my oldest boys were eighteen and fifteen.

When I stepped into the house with a bagful of groceries, my fifteen-year-old son's eyes were filled with pain. Though he attempted to talk, he choked on his words.

"What's wrong?" I recall screaming. I shook his broad shoulders, and his words tumbled out. "Aaron hanged himself."

Aaron? He was only 40 — in the prime of life — with another wife, beautiful home, good job. There had to be some mistake.

"Mom," my son said, "did you hear? Aaron hanged himself." He still didn't call his father "Dad." He used to — years ago, before we left.

Numerous thoughts congregated in my mind, but I couldn't untangle the confusion. "Is he dead?"

I watched my son lower his head and nod. Hot tears coursed down my face. Memories of early joy, coupled with abuse from Aaron, washed over me. I couldn't process it all. The combination of the past fear and present sorrow wove an unkind knot in my stomach. My throat closed, and I found it hard to swallow, much less speak. The pain I felt burst through in some kind of primal wail. Over and over again I asked myself, "Why?"

Jim put his comforting arm around me. When the pain was done with me, I allowed a veil of protection to cover me, which soon turned into depression.

The depression took a toll on me, beginning with forgetting to go to doctors. Names disappeared from memory. I couldn't follow a recipe, and I certainly couldn't be with people. So, when Jim asked me to go to a reunion, I panicked.

I became hysterical and wept uncontrollably. "Don't make me go!" I screamed. The rage that had been bottled up for years broke through like pent-up water from a dam. This emotional event brought me to the side of the road later that week. As I crossed over Georgia I-85 on my way home from the store, I saw a tractor-trailer coming toward me at full speed. Self-pity grabbed me by the throat. Tears rolled down my cheeks. No one cares if I live or die. It would be so easy. All I have to do is swerve in front of that truck.

The truck came straight at me, its back wheels kicking up dust. I gripped the steering wheel tightly, trying to get my nerve up. But the truck roared past, shaking my car. By that time, my hands were trembling, as I realized how close I'd come to taking my own life.

As the sky split open and raindrops drummed on my windshield tears streamed down my face. "Oh, God, please help me," I begged.

Incredible peace flooded my car — God's peace that passes all understanding. I sat there for a long time, before I knew what I had to do.

I had to find help. Within a week or so, I started going to a Christian counselor. As I had hoped, my momentary thought of suicide was just that. In counseling, I understood more about my father in heaven and how much he cares for me.

One day, after Jim and I had started morning devotions at home, God spoke to me through 1 John 3:1, *"How great is the love the Father has lavished on us, that we should be called children of God! And that is what we are!"* (Author's Paraphrase) How wonderful it is to know that God loves me as His child. Whenever I feel I'm slipping back into a depressed state, I can say, "I am a child of God, and nothing can hurt or defeat me."

I recall getting up in the early morning hours a few months later, marveling at the first light of dawn peeking over the horizon. Unlike the rainy day I had sat in my car trembling in fear, I was now alive again, for the first time in years. Warming my hands on my mug, I watched dazzling shades of pink and lavender dance across the sky. What joy filled my heart and soul as a distinct feeling of God's abundant peace washed over me — and I basked in His infinite love.

25

Still Afloat

Toni Armstrong Sample

In an article titled "Where the Wind Blew" I told the story of our courting and the proposal of marriage by my husband, Dave. He proposed quite unexpectedly, on his sailboat, "Soiree" (which, translated, means *evening party*) on a 4th of July holiday weekend. But "Where the Wind Blew" didn't tell what happened next.

After David pulled me into his arms, following my squeal of "Yes" to his proposal, his next words were, "When should we do this?" He meant, when should we get married.

Without even taking a breath I answered, "Now."

"Now?"

"Yes. Wasn't that your question? Should we, this weekend, sail east, west, north or get married? I opted for getting married. So, let's do it now."

"How do we make that happen?" I could tell he was more than a little surprised by my words.

"Well, I know that Tennessee has wedding chapels, and they don't have a three day wait period like they do here. Let's fly to Tennessee and get married today. I think there could be nothing more romantic than eloping. It's not like we haven't been dating for several years. We certainly don't need a long engagement to know how much we love each other. So, let's do it now."

He wrapped his arms around me, embracing me in a long and satisfying hug. He held me close and whispered in my ear, "Moments like this one are exactly why I love you so much. You are so crazy, so delightful, and so very decisive." We pulled apart, looked at each other, and laughed. This was going to be a day we would surely never forget. We were on a boat, so what better place to have a Titanic Moment. We weren't in peril, and we weren't sinking; we were headed for the greatest journey of our lives.

We motored back to our slip at the Erie Yacht Club, tied the boat and left everything we had loaded for the weekend, except the cat, on board. We took the cat to my mom and dad's house, so they could babysit my "Becky Girl." We told them that we had decided not to take the cat with us this time. We did not reveal our plans.

Dave threw some clothes in his duffle, and called to secure flight tickets to Nashville. He also called the Opryland Hotel and got us rooms. I packed, throwing in a cute flowered day dress, heels, my makeup and grooming essentials, changed into traveling clothes, and was quickly ready to leave for the airport. We were in the air within four hours of his 7:00 A.M. proposal.

Standing at the check-in desk at the hotel, we announced to the clerk that we were in Nashville to get married, that day, if possible. He said he'd arrange everything. We were to go to our rooms, get ready, and report back to the desk by 3:00 P.M., which gave us an hour to prepare for one of the biggest moments in our life.

When we arrived back at the front desk, holding hands and shaking just a little, a cab was waiting to take us to City Hall for the license. City Hall took no time at all. Our cabbie waited. He then took us to a chapel, with a real pastor, who performed a Christian service.

Every time I look at our wedding picture I am filled with happiness and a warmth that spreads through my entire body. There we are, as informal as all get out; me holding a borrowed silk flower bridal bouquet in my floral day dress, and Dave in dress pants, a short sleeved shirt and no tie. The cabbie was our witness.

The pastor spoke these words (paraphrased) from the Holy Bible — 1st Corinthians, Chapter 13 — the love chapter. "Love is patient and kind, does not envy or boast, is not self-seeking or easily angered. Love keeps no record of wrongs and does not delight in evil. Love rejoices in truth. Love protects, trusts, and perseveres. Love never fails."

Since our wedding I have read and reread those words many

times. They are often used at weddings but, as I have grown in the love of God, I have also become more aware of how those words were given, by God, to guide us in every one of our relationships.

On the ride back to the hotel Dave's arm was around my shoulders as he hugged me tightly. I felt safe and secure. Dave's smile had never been bigger. In his eyes, I saw joy and love. I hoped that he could see the very same emotions on my face, for I knew that if Dave had not been holding me tightly, that I would surely fly, much like Rose exclaimed when Jack held her on the bow of the *Titanic*.

The Concierge was waiting for us when we entered the lobby. "We have moved your things to the Bridal Suite," he said with a smile. "It is our gift to you, with no charge for the upgrade." We were flabbergasted at this generous gift to us, first-time guests of the hotel. The luxurious penthouse suite was on the top floor. We stood at the huge wall of glass, holding each other in disbelief of this windfall, as we looked down at the terrarium floor below. The curtains were closed by remote control, which frankly amazed me; and the room contained fresh flowers, fruit, chocolates, and a tray with glasses and Champagne.

I was giddy with the knowledge that this morning I was a widowed single lady, and tonight I was married. Now, provided by the courtesy of a very generous hotel, my husband and I were enjoying this very special first night of our honeymoon.

The next day we took the paddleboat to downtown Nashville, walked the streets holding hands, ate a wonderful lunch and later took a taxi to the airport for our flight home on July 4th. As the plane descended, and Erie came into view, fireworks lit the sky in every direction. They were celebrating our country's separation and ensuing independence, while Dave and I were celebrating becoming one through our union of Holy Matrimony.

It was the most memorable holiday weekend of my life.

And, until Dave's death in 2008, for twenty-five years we were still afloat.

26

Free-Falling Without a Parachute

David Brannock

If at first you don't succeed, avoid skydiving.

Parachuting from a plane at 14,000 feet isn't on my bucket list. White knuckling the sides of the open door as I fight to keep down lunch isn't my idea of fun. The promised adrenaline rush of a free fall and canopy ride has yet to override my fear of landing in the obituary column.

You might understand why I threw a fit the first time the Lord took me skydiving into faith. For a while, life seemed like a free fall with no parachute. Until that experience, I thought I trusted God. But then the belly flop I feared threatened to materialize.

While I was busy making plans over the years, God was equipping me for this jump. In college, I loved the summer I taught math classes at my old high school. After a brief stint in public accounting, I prepared to teach at a small college. During my last semester of grad school, a private liberal-arts college offered me a full-time position as an assistant professor of accounting.

With my wedding scheduled the week after graduation, I thought my life was set. I pictured my pretty wife helping me organize my bookshelves and hang my diplomas in a faculty office with my name on the door. Once I settled in, I envisioned eager students seeking counsel about classes or life.

When my fiancée and I brought this offer to God, dark clouds roiled our spirits. We prayed, "If this is the right job, ease our apprehension. If not, increase our uneasiness." The Lord elevated our turmoil. After I turned down my supposed dream job, God cocooned us in peace.

Next I interviewed with a company in the Tennessee city where my fiancée worked. A second interview placed me in consideration for two openings. Shortly before graduation, I learned two other candidates filled those positions.

Uncertainty attacked my faith. "God, where are you? What are you doing?"

A still, small voice whispered to my heart. *Trust me.*

Through prayer I became persuaded I'd be employed by Labor Day. A persistent feeling entered my spirit about this date. On Father's Day I shared my firm conviction with Mom and Dad. They asked, "How do you know for sure?"

I pointed to my new bride. "How do you *know* when you've fallen in love? You just do."

Yet, two months after I bragged on the Lord to my parents, doubt replaced certainty. Every employer I applied to either said no or never responded. Now I greeted each sunrise with greater skepticism about God's plans and purposes.

I resented this forced skydive of faith. Out of options, I felt like I had no parachute. And this wasn't Hollywood where I could take my shirt and shoelaces and build one on the way down.

Before dawn on Monday, August 19, I slipped out of bed and plopped on the couch in our one-bedroom apartment. An angry prayer started my day. "Have you checked the calendar lately? No prospects remain and Labor Day is just two weeks away."

I'd submitted my education and career to God. By faith, I passed up a big opportunity. Now, three months after I gained a wife and a diploma, we were treading financial water, going nowhere fast. Once my student loan repayments started, her income alone couldn't sustain us.

On this muggy August morning, fourteen days from Labor Day, the ground raced closer. I stared at the ceiling, blinking back hot tears, and hissed. "Why are you letting this happen? Why won't you step in and help me? Why don't I matter to you?"

Trust me.

My pulse spiked when the mail arrived. I pulled out a stack of bills and ads. The next day the mail carrier brought more disappointment. I began to brace for impact.

Later that week the phone rang. We didn't have caller ID, so I grimaced at the prospect of another telemarketer's spiel. I answered politely, ready to end the sales pitch. But my heart pounded when the caller identified herself as Dean of Business at a nearby college.

The dean invited me to her office to discuss an immediate opening for an adjunct accounting instructor. It wasn't a full-time position. Our kitchen table would double as my office. Still, as my feet prepared to land in a level field, I thanked God for the grace to fulfill my dream of teaching at a small school while my wife kept her job.

In that moment, I realized I wasn't outfitted with a parachute because God wore it for both of us. All along I'd been part of a tandem skydive. Certified instructors recommend that first-time students make a tandem jump instead of a solo jump. During the free fall, faith had securely connected me to my Instructor's harness.

Oddly enough, after not working all summer, I'd teach my first class on September 2.

Monday, September 2.

Labor Day.

O Lord Almighty,
happy are those who trust in you.

Psalm 84:12
(Author's Paraphrase)

27

A Smooth-Sailing Night

Rebecca Carpenter

Although neither of us verbalized it, Alan and I knew it would be the last birthday we would celebrate together. Recent events let us know his time was short. At his pulmonologist's office after the doctor listened to his lungs, Alan asked, "How much time do I have?"

With a solemn face the doctor said, "Six months."

We knew that his breathing was more labored and his strength waning from the idiopathic pulmonary fibrosis, but I was not prepared for that prognosis. I wondered why Alan even asked. The doctor's words cut deeply into my heart.

My eyes blinked hard to keep the tears from flowing. Deep breaths helped calm my racing heart. Alan remained stoic.

While the nurse got a wheelchair for Alan, I numbly walked to get the car. A few months earlier, he had given up driving because of his fatigue and slow reflexes. When I pulled up to the door, my formerly active, muscular husband waited for me in a wheelchair.

Later that day, a hospice worker arrived at our home to admit him into their program. A nurse came with more information. A man brought oxygen canisters and a condenser. In one day our lives changed dramatically.

For two weeks we tried to adjust to our new lifestyle. Days before my birthday, Alan announced that he made reservations at a romantic restaurant to celebrate. From the time we started dating, each year he took me out for a birthday dinner.

Because of his worsening health, he rested all day on my birthday so he would have enough energy to celebrate. When I gently told him we didn't have to go, he said, "I want to do it."

With no handicapped spaces available near the restaurant that evening, I dropped him off at the curb in front of the restaurant. Tears threatened as I circled the area, searching for a parking spot. As I walked alone through the dark, I thought of the years he had taken care of me, and how now, his illness had reversed our roles. Neither of us liked the changes, but we had learned to adapt.

The nagging question in my mind returned. *Will this be my last birthday with Alan?*

He carried his portable oxygen tank as we walked into the darkened dining room. At our table for two, glittery birthday confetti sparkled on the black tablecloth next to a simple white card with our name printed on it. The special touches welcomed us and made me smile. I forced the intruding question away.

Our attentive waiter recited the menu and answered our questions. Alan and I talked quietly while we waited for our meal. Only a few diners sat near us in the small, elegant dining room. No one else knew this would be our only visit together to the award-winning restaurant.

We savored every bite of each creatively decorated dish. Normally, we skipped dessert, but Alan urged me to choose one for our special occasion. He declined to order one for himself but took a bite of my luscious crème brûlée. Our sumptuous meals delighted us. The chef deserved his awards.

Even though the dinner didn't eliminate our concerns, we received several blessings. Alan's oxygen tank, taken there as a precaution, remained unused on the floor because he could breathe easily. His taste buds, usually dulled by medications, allowed him to fully appreciate his meal that night. For one evening, we shoved aside thoughts of his impending death and enjoyed my birthday. No one around us knew of our struggles. We talked and laughed like we had on previous birthdays. What a marvelous birthday blessing I received.

Alan no longer dines with me on my birthday, but gratefulness fills me each time I remember the special night of smooth sailing, and the life of love we had together.

28

Pray About It

Phil Gladden

My wife Ruth often makes the comment, "What would you do without me."

She says it in jest, but my answer is always the same. "I would wilt away."

Ruth is one of the most honest upbeat good-hearted people you would ever want to know. She treats everyone she meets like they were old friends. She is the love of my life.

About a month ago, Ruth had chest pains and woke me up in the middle of the night. We went to the emergency room. She was given some blood thinners and then sent back home.

Three nights later the same thing happened, so we headed to Saint Joseph's Hospital. After several uncomfortable tests, they told us Ruth has a large mass that extended from her lung and either into her heart or just behind it.

We were told that doing a biopsy would be too dangerous because she might not wake up. They felt sure it was likely cancer that had returned. She had survived Non-Hodgkin's Lymphoma and had been cancer-free for eight years.

They sent her for a cardiac MRI and a PET scan to see if surgery, followed by chemotherapy would be possible. Our greatest fear was that the tumor had infiltrated the heart and would be inoperable.

Prayer chains went up in our church, throughout our family and even by friends we barely know on Facebook. We spent the following three weeks praying, crying, and hugging each other, but the thing that is surprising, neither of us were afraid.

We are sixty-five years old, and are truly amazed at how blessed we have been. So many of our friends died at young ages, many from senseless actions that were no fault of their own. Some lives ended violently. We think about other families that face these same trials, but with a six-year-old, rather than sixty-five-year-olds, and we pray for them.

We had prepared for the worst, and were ready to face whatever was in front of us with strength we gained over a lifetime, and by the power that comes from knowing a loving God. He always has a plan and his is always the best plan, even if we don't always understand it.

We drove to Lexington for answers, armed with a strong faith as well as a love for each other. We sat for thirty minutes in the doctor's waiting room, feeling that every second crawled past. Then we spent another fifteen in the examination room. Most of that time was spent in silent prayer and with me rubbing Ruth's back and shoulders. All of a sudden, the door swung open and in walked the doctor and his assistant. The doctor sat down and asked a few preliminary questions. He then leaned back and began to speak.

"Well, Mrs. Gladden, we sent you for a MRI and CAT scan. I have to tell you, I'm more than a little surprised. I didn't see any abnormalities at all. There was a little inflammation in the lymph nodes, but even that was a fraction of what we saw before. There is no mass in or around the heart. I can't do a biopsy because there is nothing to do it on. In fact, I had to check to see if I was looking at the correct test, because the results were so different."

We left the doctor's office with tears of joy in our eyes and praises to God, who is the ultimate healer, in our hearts.

Now let me be clear. If you are someone who doesn't believe in God . . . If you are someone who this world has convinced that prayer has no power . . . If that is what you truly believe, then you need to meet a miracle, whose name is Ruth Gladden. She is the love of my life, and I thank God for her every day. And I am here to declare, there is a Healer who is without limits and he is my God. I hope you get to know him.

Until next time . . . Just pray about it.

29

Pray Jesus, Me

Lydia E. Harris

The day I learned our fifteen-month-old grandson, Owen, needed surgery for two holes in his heart, I cried myself to sleep. When I awoke the next morning, tears still ran down my cheeks. Later, when my son called, I told him, "I feel so terrible that you have to go through this scary time with Owen." I wished I could somehow shield this young family from the stress and uncertainty of what lay ahead.

Two months later, I accompanied my son and daughter-in-law to the medical appointment where we learned the grim details of Owen's upcoming open-heart surgery. My heart ached when I heard what my little grandson would go through.

"We'll stop his heart and put him on a heart and lung machine," the surgeon said. I tried to reassure myself that all these procedures were routine. But as I talked with my son later, he asked the nagging, unspoken question that loomed in my mind: "What if he dies?"

A few weeks before Owen's surgery, while driving home from a meeting, I heard a familiar hymn on the radio. As I listened to the melody of, "All to Jesus, I Surrender," a sob from deep within burst out, and I said aloud, "Oh no, Lord, I have to give you Owen!" I cried the rest of the way home as I struggled to place Owen in God's hands.

When the date for Owen's open-heart surgery neared, I wanted to give him the best gift I could — lots of prayer. So I arranged a 24-hour prayer circle for him during the time of his surgery. Family, friends, and even people who had never met Owen, chose hours of the day and night to surround him with prayer.

On the day of surgery, my husband and I awoke early and met Owen and his parents at the hospital. Owen's parents dressed him in a little hospital gown, and a medical assistant examined him. Owen looked so fragile at just seventeen pounds. I got to hold Owen and gave him a final hug. But I didn't want to let him go. I felt like a traitor when I watched as my unsuspecting little grandson was handed to the smiling nurse. He whisked Owen away from us before he could cry.

The door shut behind them.

Then we waited and prayed. During this uncertain time, I was comforted in knowing Owen was surrounded with prayer around the clock. I knew one or more people had agreed to pray for him every hour for twenty-four hours.

After the surgery, Owen cried nonstop for hours, and I cried, too. He looked so pathetic connected to all those machines and tubes. Thankfully, I could update the prayer warriors by email and ask them to fervently keep praying for our little grandson.

God answered the many prayers of family and friends. Owen recovered quickly with no complications. To everyone's surprise, he came home after three days instead of five to seven. And in a few days, he again scooted around on his little fire truck.

A year later, on the anniversary of Owen's successful surgery, we celebrated together as a family and thanked God for our spunky, happy two-year-old. Owen entertained us with his requests for, "More coupons please," which meant he wanted salad croutons. The dinner ended with Owen and his four-year-old sister singing a Sunday school chorus they knew, "Hosanna to the King of Kings."

Although before his surgery Owen seemed too tired to even crawl, before long he could run, jump, and climb. He also loved to pray. Sometimes he would fall down on his hands and knees and bow his head to pray. Other times, before meals, he would say, "Pray Jesus, me."

Now, years later, looking at our enthusiastic seventh-grade grandson, I rejoice and thank God that he hears and answers prayer.

"Call to me and I will answer you".

Jeremiah 33:3 NIV

30

It Is Well

Mirjam Budarz and Dr. Timo Budarz

My beloved sister Liisa died last year in Finland after a long battle, first with a stroke and then with Alzheimer's. This is the letter my son Timo sent to his Finnish cousins:

Dearest Ccousins,

Last Sunday morning I heard the news of your mother and my aunt passing away. I got the message on my phone early in the morning, so I lay in bed and looked at the picture I had been sent of her only days earlier. As I looked at the photo of her failing emaciated body, I had a crisis of faith. I lay there wondering if there was a chance that her lifetime of faith ended with her last breath. I wondered if your mother — her character and soul — was anywhere at all right then.

I knew what my faith told me, and I knew what I wanted to believe, and I was thinking of those things as I rose from bed and made breakfast for the boys and a cup of coffee for myself.

Wanting to believe is very different than believing, and yet I knew that one thing I needed to do that morning was to send condolences to my mother for losing her closest sister and friend.

I picked up my phone and the only thing that came to mind were the words of an old hymn from the 1870s written by a man who had lost everything. He had lost his two-year-old son, then lost extensive property in the historic Chicago fire, then sent his family ahead of himself to Europe on vacation but the ship sank and he lost 4 daughters while his wife survived. Traveling alone to meet her and passing near the place where his daughters had drowned in the ocean, he penned the words of the hymn "It Is Well With My Soul."

That hymn came to mind because it is about final destinies. The man who wrote it believed that life here is only the beginning of a longer story whose end was already written, and that ultimately, it was well with his soul.

So I wondered that morning if the faith your mother possessed was indeed true. Was it well with her soul? I didn't want to betray my confidence, and simply wrote my mother a text message that morning saying, "Sorry. It is well with her soul. She was my favorite aunt, probably because she was in character similar to my mama."

I then sat down at the piano and played the hymn over and over while wondering about her soul and hoping I would find confirmation in a concrete way at church that morning. So on the way to church I knew what I wanted. I also knew that our church doesn't play hymns. They only play modern, progressive music. But I wanted to hear that hymn. In some sense I needed to hear it.

The music part of the service ended with me being disappointed. As the sermon went on I thought maybe there could be a message of confirmation in it. The young preacher gave a good message, but nothing I'd say was a confirmation. I was feeling down and distracted.

Then came his concluding remarks. He blessed the congregation and then in a way that didn't even seem to flow from the content of the message said, "And now, please listen to the words of this song. It is called, 'It Is Well.'" I began to weep as the familiar words were sung.

God, who orchestrates all things, found a way to inspire a young preacher in southern California to make a song request of his musicians that was really to commemorate the life of an old woman in Finland who had passed away hours earlier, and to reassure her doubting nephew that his faith is not without foundation and that neither was hers.

I am sorry for your loss, but I can confidently say that it is well with her soul.

God bless you both,

Timo

Mirjam's note:

As my son, Eerik, and I traveled to the funeral in Finland, we visited Israel. In Jerusalem, in the House of Prayer, a sheet of paper was given to us as we left. On it were the lyrics of that same hymn. Also, Timo had another confirmation, as he biked to Huntington Beach, the same song was being played there by a surfer evangelist.

It is well.

My sister Liisa was a special person, a poet, a gift giver and lover of God and people. The Holy Spirit was so active, that at my niece's house after Liisa's funeral four people accepted Christ, and two other persons as well through "chance" encounters.

"I assure you, anyone who believes in me already has eternal life."

Jesus in John 6:47 NLT

31

That Dirty Ol' Thing?

Alice Klies

One morning I thumbed through the pages of my Bible and my eyes fell on this familiar passage: *Put off your old self, which belongs to your former manner of life and is corrupt though deceitful desires . . . be renewed in the spirit of your mind and . . . put on the new self, created after the likeness of God in true righteousness and holiness.* (Ephesians 4:22-24 ESV)

I felt like someone had just thrown cold water in my face . . . my new self? How was I new?

My pastor often shared with people that they could pray to bring Jesus into their hearts and become new in Him. I've been a believer since I was a child, but as an adult I had read only snippets of a Bible. When I joined a church that encouraged me to read a Bible, my life changed.

I read the passage again. *Yes, I thought, I have changed. The more I take time to study scripture I have realized I'm often guilty of pride, worry, judgment and a multitude of toxic behaviors I'm trying hard to correct. I can honestly say I didn't recognize them before I read God's word.*

I scrunched myself into the soft cushions of my couch. I could see that after I had started reading a Bible, I had begun to understand what God asks of believers, that He wants our lives to conform to His ways. As I thought this I felt tingles creep up my spine because it's so hard to actively show love to someone who has hurt me. And I remembered how difficult it was to trust that God would deliver me when I'd gone through trials I thought I'd never get through.

Am I holy and righteous? Egad no! However, when I tried to digest this passage and analyze it, I saw I'm certainly more aware of my old self and my ability today to be more Christ like.

When I see someone dressed a little differently and start TO judge him, I'm able to stop myself and feel the Holy Spirit admonish me. I know I'm to be full of God's love and actively show it to everyone I see.

My insides moan as soon as I've screeched at the driver who just cut me off. I'm able to look skyward and say, "I'm sorry God." I pray for that person, "Please God, don't let him hurt someone with his wild driving."

I'm able to forgive because I know God asks this of us. I honestly have trouble sometime forgetting the hurt but I no longer let it stew in my heart.

I've always been a "Martha," in that I feel a need to be in control. This is an area of my life where God thumped me on the top of my head. He reminds me daily . . . He is in control! So, yes, I've asked forgiveness in this area a lot.

I thumbed through more scripture.

"I rejoice, not because you were grieved, but because you were grieved into repenting. For you felt a godly grief, so that you suffered no loss through us. For godly grief produces a repentance that leads to salvation without regret, whereas worldly grief produces death (2 Corinthians 7:11 ESV).

Yep, it's tough in today's world to truly say one doesn't have to repent daily because there are so many worldly things to tempt us. My nightly prayers include asking for forgiveness; sometimes I ask to be forgiven for the same thing I asked for the week before. Talk about feeling guilty! Am I someone who has changed, thrown out the old self?

Yes, I do grieve when I repeat the same wrong I've asked forgiveness for the week before. Each time I'm genuinely very sorry and yes, I've felt awful for days. This passage was harder to read because a sin should be abolished, not repeated. Then I rationalized, "It's just an exaggeration, not a lie. Sometimes I stretch the truth in order to keep from hurting someone's feelings."

The Holy Spirit whispered in my ear, "An untruth is a lie no matter how you stretch it."

I hung my head. I closed my Bible. My mind raced. *It's not easy to be a Christian. It's hard work to remain faithful to God's word. I know I'm not alone when I fail but I also know for sure that God forgives my failures as long as I recognize them, confess them and move on to try to follow in His footsteps as best as I can.*

I think of the adage, "Don't throw the baby out with the bath water." That comes from the days before running water in the house. The entire family bathed in the same tub and by the time the baby had a bath, the water might be so dirty you might not see the baby in it.

Most importantly, that morning, I was sure I'd thrown out most of my old self (dirty water). I had an assurance I'd live forever in heaven with our Savior. I sipped my coffee, pulled my Bible (the baby) close to my chest and eagerly opened it to another thought-provoking piece of scripture — such as John 7:38, and became clean with the Living Water.

32

Special Delivery

Lt. Col. Robert Robeson

Nearly five decades have come and gone, yet one moment in time continues to play back through my mind at regular intervals. It's like the music of a beloved love song from one's early dating years. Unique. Inspiring. Unforgettable.

May 9, 1970. Another oppressively hot and humid Asian afternoon was drawing to a close for our helicopter medical evacuation crew of four near Da Nang, South Vietnam. I was an aircraft commander and also commander of the 236th Medical Detachment (Helicopter Ambulance) located at Red Beach on the southern shore of Da Nang Harbor.

My medic for the day was First Lieutenant Ron Reidenbaugh, a close friend who also functioned as my administrative medical officer on the ground. I'd tagged him with the nickname "The Mauler," because of his size and aggressive outlook on life. He was a young man you liked right away, perpetually smiling and always full of humor. At 6-2 and 235 muscular pounds, he was an imposing figure. He'd been a defensive end in football at Kent State University before being commissioned as an officer.

In the previous month, the thirteen pilots in our unit had experienced having sixteen helicopters shot up or shot down. We'd gone through our authorized inventory of six helicopters nearly three times. Our flight crews had been stretched to the maximum. Mauler had volunteered to fly as a medic (due to his extensive medical training at Kent State) to give a few of our enlisted medics a breather.

We had just completed a number of difficult medical evacuations of wounded South Vietnamese soldiers from remote jungle locations. Now we were lifting off from our field-site aid station at Landing Zone Hawk Hill. Two ambulatory patients and a youthful, pregnant Vietnamese woman on a litter were being flown to the Vietnamese hospital in Da Nang.

It was a thirty-six-mile flight. A few minutes after takeoff, a call came over our FM radio. We were asked to evacuate an Australian civilian from the coastal town of Hoi An. His ankle had been crushed by a heavy fifty-five-gallon drum. We made the pickup en route and flew north along the South China Sea toward Da Nang.

After the second takeoff, Mauler noticed that our pregnant patient was beginning to stir. Her eyes had been closed. Now she was alert and the old mama-san accompanying her was pointing and attempting to communicate in high-pitched Vietnamese.

"I think the aid station was a bit off on its estimate," Mauler said. "Doc told me she wasn't going to deliver for a couple of days." He had a rare frown on his face. "Can you go any faster? I've never delivered a baby before."

"Me, either," I chided him. "You're the one who volunteered to fly as a medic."

I turned in my armored seat and glanced at the fragile-looking young woman lying on a litter covered with yesterday's bloodstains. We were at 2,000 feet with the cargo doors open. Her long black hair was blowing in the refreshing slipstream. Black peasant garments were tucked in at the waist and knotted.

"Can you go any faster?" Mauler repeated. "She's in labor."

"It's redlined," I replied.

Mauler was bent hunchbacked before her litter. He was silhouetted against the light green of the South China Sea, behind and far below.

Our rotor blades beat against the air and wore down the minutes as I initiated a rapid descent and approached Marble Mountain. These rugged, triple-peaks marked the southeastern outskirts of Da Nang. We were on the deck, now, about five feet above waves gently breaking on the white sandy beach beneath our skids. I felt that exhilarating sensation of tremendous speed that one doesn't experience at altitude. Doing 120 knots (about 140 mph) this close to the ground, as our Lycoming jet turbine engine rumbled away behind us, felt like Warp Factor Ninety.

Normally, during daylight hours, all Vietnamese patients were taken to the Vietnamese Province Hospital in the center of Da Nang. As aircraft commander, though, I'd already made the decision to take her directly to the U.S. Army 95th Evacuation Hospital. It was located on China Beach, touching the South China Sea, to the east. Here she would get the best and quickest medical care available.

"We're not going to make it," Mauler said matter-of-factly over the intercom.

"I'll call ahead and have a nurse standing by on the pad at the 95th," I replied.

Everyone in the aircraft was suddenly concerned for this mother-to-be and the new life about to be born into a war zone. Glancing over my shoulder, I was amazed to see that her face was not distorted by pain. Instead, her features appeared to convey peacefulness and tenderness. These were qualities not often observed by soldiers accustomed to the danger, devastation and death of everyday combat situations.

The next words that I heard, coming a short time later, were those of our crew chief. "Congratulations, sir. We've got us a girl."

When I turned around to see, Mauler's hands were covered with blood. (In those days, no one used rubber gloves in combat outside of a medical facility.) He was cradling a tiny Oriental infant. Those arms that had effortlessly knocked two-hundred-pound men around on the gridiron now tenderly held this fragile child. Then, like Ben Casey from some old TV rerun, he gently patted that small bottom with an oversized palm. We all heard the first sharp wail of new life above the noise of our rotors and jet engine.

I thought back to other days, to previous moments . . . mystical moments. Those were times when we'd rescued someone from under enemy fire we'd been seeking for a long time. I experienced now what I'd felt then — reverence. Suddenly it hits you and you discover in an instant of awareness how wonderful a human life is, no matter where in the world it's located.

There was a slight breeze, fresh from the sea, wafting its burden of salt and faint scent of fish. I cranked our bird into a hard left turn and hairy flare at the same time for the hospital pad over gentle green waves.

An American nurse met the aircraft as we scattered a group of medics playing volleyball on one corner of the concrete landing pad. She smiled at Mauler as he walked beside the gurney that wheeled his patients toward the emergency room. As they passed my window, I caught the young mother's eye and made a circle with my thumb and forefinger. She reacted to this international sign with a shy smile and managed a slight wave of a thin hand.

The medics playing volleyball moved closer to the gurney and seemed to sense what was written on all of our faces. For this distinct moment in time, at least, we were a part of life. Then, without any coaching or explanation, they began to applaud the young woman, her newborn and their bulky escort.

A few minutes later, Mauler ran back to our bird and gave the volleyball players the thumbs-up signal. It was as though he'd just sacked an opposing quarterback and was acknowledging enthusiastic support from his hometown fans.

After shutting down at our airfield, Mauler walked the eighth-of-a-mile to my hootch with me. His war, to that point, had been doing administrative tasks on the ground and in an office where lives weren't in constant jeopardy. For a few days, then, he'd discovered that combat flying could be exciting, dangerous, often fearful and yet extremely fulfilling because of the opportunities to impact lives one-on-one.

"For once I feel like I did something worthwhile," Mauler admitted. "It can be a real kick, can't it?"

I nodded. After ten months in daily combat — and having flown over 900 missions to that point — I understood what he meant. It's a feeling few people will ever know under such primitive and hostile conditions. He'd been responsible for preserving the lives of a number of wounded allied soldiers earlier that morning. Now he'd been intimately involved in welcoming a new traveler onto our spinning ball of clay. That's a good day's work for anyone.

For the record, there will always be one medical evacuation mission that I remember as being unique in a year of combat flying. It's that springtime moment in May that involved universal involvement above Da Nang. That's when citizens of three different nations cared and shared together for the common good of the newest miracle on our planet. It reminded me a little of another baby born nearly two-thousand years before in Bethlehem. That, too, was a peasant birth that relied on the kindness of strangers during difficult and dangerous times.

My generation's war has long since been over. (It's been over half an average life span since that aerial birth and the time Mauler and I last saw each other. He now lives in Ohio.) I've often prayed that this baby girl escaped the demise of her country a few years later. Hopefully, her family made it to a safe shore somewhere. Every child has potential, is important and we can never predict the impact one specific life will have on our world.

I often replay that mission in my mind. Now I realize it was a victory of life in the midst of death. It was another fresh beginning to inspire those who were still trapped in the throes of war's winter of discontent. That baby's birth was a solitary and unique rose that bloomed without fanfare in God's springtime garden in Southeast Asia to provide a sense of hope for us all. It was a "special delivery" package I doubt any of us will ever forget.

Postscript

In previous wars, crew chiefs of fighter aircraft would take pride in denoting the number of planes shot down by their pilots. The usual method was by painting a small replica of the enemy's flag on the side of the aircraft. A few days after our flight, I went down to our flight line to preflight my aircraft. On the pilots' doors, on each side of the helicopter, our crew chief had someone paint a small symbol — a white stork with a tiny baby suspended in a diaper from the stork's bill. I guess he felt it was important to make a point of keeping score.

33

A Time for Everything

Beverly Hill McKinney

I have some good news and some bad news," our realtor told us over the phone. "The good news is that I have a buyer for the house but the bad news is that they want more concessions."

Oh, Lord, how will we get those funds back in time?

I think back on that time and realize how God taught me to trust his perfect timing. It was the summer of 2003. We were driving to Vancouver, Washington to attend a family reunion. Since we were driving from Southern California, we stopped for the night at a motel right off the freeway in small Southern Oregon town. We checked in, ate a meal, then drove around the community.

We liked what we saw that evening and decided to come back the next summer and look for a possible future retirement home.

Since we had a relative who was a realtor, we contacted her and she not only agreed to look for us but also offered to let us stay in her guest house.

The next summer, we arrived and were excited that we not only had a lovely place to stay but she had already looked over properties for us so we could begin our search the next day. Going out the next day, we looked at some rural property but the houses all needed lots of work. At that point, we decided to go to a nearby community. However, our realtor said a home had just become available that morning and since we were in the neighborhood, why not stop by and look at it. As we parked outside the house, we called the listing realtor and she gave us permission to look at the property.

Walking into the house, my husband, Jim, said, "This is our house." We were not planning on buying anything on this trip but he felt that this was the place for us. We returned to the real estate office and wrote up an offer for the house. Our mortgage company approved a loan for the asking price. The offer was accepted and we spent the rest of the week touring the surrounding area, excited about the prospect that this would be our new home.

I wanted to put a large down payment on the house so our payments would not be as hard to manage. I called my retirement investment counselor and asked if I had any money I could use for a down payment. He told me I had a large amount I could put down. However, it would have to be replaced within 60 days or we would be taxed on that entire amount. Since our home in Southern California was not yet for sale, we hurried home and put it on the market.

Jim put in his retirement papers and since I had already retired, we began to pack for our move to Oregon. Our house in Southern California was only a few miles from the beach so we knew it should sell quickly. However, as the move date neared, we'd had many looking but no offers.

We moved to Oregon on faith that the Lord would provide a buyer for our home. The days were nearing the time for our down payment to be put back in my retirement account. Finally, a buyer was found but they had some options they wanted before signing. As the days counted down and they continued to make demands, I began to question the Lord and ask what we should do?

I prayed earnestly for the funds to come in before the 60 days. Our relator finally called and said the escrow had closed and our money was on the way. On day 58 the money arrived and I arranged for immediate repayment of the loan. I smiled as I realized how the Lord was trying to teach me to trust in him.

The Lord knew that the time was right for us to buy then instead of at a later date. Looking back, we realized that if we had not bought our home at that time, we would not have been able to as the housing market went into a slump and the property we had in Southern California fell below what we had sold it for.

Despite my doubting, I realized God does care where we live, and his timing is always right.

34

How to Organize a 24-Hour Circle of Prayer

Lydia E. Harris

During a personal or family crisis, around-the-clock prayers build a solid wall of protection and comfort. To enlist a 24-hour prayer circle for a loved one, take these steps:

- Contact family and friends at least a week before with information about the surgery or need, and invite them to pray (email works well). Your message could read: "Please select an hour in the day or night (PDT) when you will stand in the gap to pray. It's fine if several choose the same time." List the time slots around the clock (e.g., March 21: 7–8 A.M., 8–9 A.M., midnight–1 A.M.). Encourage those in other time zones to choose night hours when those in your area would be asleep.
- After people sign up, email everyone a list of who is praying when. If not all of them know each other, include a short identification by each name (e.g., Susie's aunt, friend of Susie's grandma).
- The day before surgery, email the prayer warriors a prayer guide with specific requests for the patient, his/her family, and the medical team. You could also include specific scriptures to pray for the patient and family.
- During the patient's recovery, email periodic updates.
- A few weeks after surgery, send thank-you notes (email or regular mail) to all who prayed.
- If possible, plan a celebration to thank God for answered prayers.

A circle of prayer can be used for any crisis, not only a medical one. As we band together in prayer, we show God we are serious about our concern, and we appeal to God Almighty, the source of power, to help the person in need. Then later, together we can rejoice in God's answers, no matter what the outcome.

Is there someone you can you wrap in love through a circle of prayer?

35

Why Am I Here?

Diana Leagh Matthews

As I approached the hill on my evening walk, the intensity to make it up the hill was matched by my prayers.

"Lord, what is my purpose? Why am I here?" My soul cried out for answers, but this was far from the first time I'd asked this question. I had begged God to reveal that to me since I'd returned to my mother's home following an abusive relationship. It was a question to which I wondered if I would ever discover the answer.

I had been lost and adrift at sea with no purpose for too long. The path had led to destruction, pain, heartache and unfulfilled dreams.

I had returned to my family, broken in spirit and body. Only time would heal my wounds and allow me to piece the fractures together into a new and better picture. I had been through intensive counseling in the last year, but knew I still had a long way to go.

More than anything I wanted to help others and share my struggles with other women in my situation, but I had to find my own healing before I could reach out to others. I heard a voice whisper in my spirit, "You have to learn to love yourself before you can help others."

Learning to love the little girl buried deep inside of me who had been beaten down, battered and cast ashore was far from easy. I'll be honest, I've come a long way, but still struggle. But, I knew that was part of the healing process.

I longed for answers and cried out the same question day after day on my evening walk. Finally, after two more years passed, I heard a voice say, "Show my kind of love."

To some people those words would mean nothing, but to me

they took me back to another time in my life. I had been my pastor-father's pianist since I was ten years old. Daddy often ended his sermons with a song or hymn.

In the early 1990s, while I was finishing my high school years, Daddy compiled some of his favorite songs into a cantata. These were songs we had performed many times over the years. Songs that included the Gaither's "The Old Rugged Cross Made a Difference" and "I Believe in a Hill Called Mt. Calvary." "Lovest Thou Me" and the hymn, "When I Survey the Old Rugged Cross" were compiled into a cantata and accompanied by scripture. That Easter, we performed the musical together, accompanied by a slide show and communion.

Fast forward to the year 2000, and once again Daddy and I discussed dusting off the cantata he had compiled and performing it that Easter. "We will definitely perform it *next* Easter," Daddy promised. He did not have to tell me that, this Easter, he was too weak from the cancer he was battling. With sadness, we lost him before the next Easter and all I could dwell on that year was our now-extinct plans.

Three years later, the pastor where I was minister of music, longed to do something special for Easter. I mentioned the cantata, which I now had in my possession, and we agreed to the production. I made a few changes and tweaks, but maintained the essence of Daddy's vision. I had a lot riding on the production, since it was also my college internship. I even incorporated the slideshow and communion service, which added to the message of God's love through Jesus' sacrifice.

As the production date neared, and my choir prepared, I needed a name for the musical. Daddy had never provided a title for the production, but I knew it had to be something special. I began to read over the lyrics of the various songs we were using. Nothing seemed to fit. I turned about halfway through the cantata to a song written by Marijohn Wilkin. This was a song Daddy and I had performed several times in the fifteen years we performed together, but on this given day the words spoke to me in a different way.

I read over the words, which talked about Jesus showing his love on the cross. The lyrics said this love was a perfect love and only the kind of love God could show. The chorus discussed how Jesus could have called the angels to save him, but he didn't, and how they must have cried as they stood helplessly nearby. The lyrics shared that it wasn't the nails holding Jesus to the cross, but his love for mankind and that the heavens shuddered as Jesus made the ultimate sacrifice. The song ends by saying that Jesus' love is a perfect kind of love.

Something about these lyrics spoke to my heart and I decided "His Kind of Love" was the perfect title for the cantata.

Now, here I was a decade past this performance and I heard God whispering the title of this song into my heart.

"But, how do I show your kind of love?" I asked. At that time, I was still struggling to find forgiveness and move on from my own battered past.

"Love others and love yourself," the voice whispered. This wasn't easy and took a lot of work, but in time I learned to do just that. I discovered how to love myself and show love to others. On the days when I grew weary and tired, I reminded myself of the passage where Jesus said, *"Truly I tell you, whatever you did for one of the least of these brothers and sisters of mine, you did for me"* (Matthew 25:40 NIV).

As I began my own ministry, I felt those words again ringing through my head. My ministry, as well as my life purpose, is to show God's love to others.

Today, in addition to my ministry, I work as a Certified Activities Director at a skilled nursing facility. Each morning, I ask God to use me as a light for him and show his love to all those I encounter.

There are days when I'm not sure I've been successful, but then I will have someone thank me or point out a kind deed that I thought nothing about performing. That is not to say there are no challenging days. Recently in an activity, I grew so tired of the bickering between my residents that I turned to them and said, "We need to get along and love our brothers and sisters the way God wants us to" (1 John 4:21).

I realized that truth and virtue have seeped into the depths of my being and soul. I may not always get it right, but I strive to show God's kind of love to all those I come into contact with. By showing God's love, I never know how I may make a difference in someone's life, provide a kindness when it is most needed, or be a living witness for my Lord and Savior.

Showing God's love to others takes work and isn't easy, but it is definitely possible. So, the next time someone difficult comes along, ask God to reveal to you how to show his love to that person. But, be prepared. You never know what he may ask you to do and the personal sacrifice you will be required to make. However, I promise that it gets easier the more this trait is put into practice.

After all, Jesus commanded us to love one another: *"A new commandment I give to you, that you love one another: just as I have loved you, you also are to love one another. By this all people will know that you are my disciples, if you have love for one another."* (John 13:34-35 ESV)

36
Joyful Sadness

Margaret Peterson

"It's my Mom!" The cry erupted from deep within me. My body trembled and I stumbled to explain. "Dad said they got her diagnosis." I choked out the words. "It's terminal cancer."

My husband's dark eyes widened and he swallowed hard. He took the phone from my hand, replaced the receiver and pulled me into his arms. My sobs broke the prolonged silence. "Did your dad say how long she has?" I shook my head and tears spilled onto his shirt making small dark circles on the blue.

When we found out her prognosis my world spun out of control like a leaf caught in a whirlpool. My mom had less than a year to live.

I began weekend trips from San Antonio to Houston to be with my beloved mother. She and I shared our memories, our laughter and our tears. We prayed incessantly for the miracle of restored health that Mom believed could be hers.

We continued our intercession with desperation as mom's strength waned and her weight dropped away.

Confined, finally, to a hospital bed set up in the sunroom, Mom looked like a porcelain doll propped up by fluffy pillows and swaddled in colorful afghans. She took part in family activities and had countless visitors. Friends, neighbors, and church members brought flowers, gifts, food and offers of help. The pastor and his wife came by regularly and one evening the church elders arrived to pray over Mom and anoint her with oil, in accordance with James 5:14-15.

The months dragged by and Mom shriveled up like the blooms on a two week old bouquet by her bedside. Only her radiant smile in her thin, white face remained unchanged. The long, agonizing year ended and Mom was still with us. We gave the Lord our heartfelt thanks.

Six months later, on my weekend visit, she told me of a blessed experience that had occurred earlier in the week. She had been reading her Bible and praying when she felt the Lord's presence. "Although I couldn't see Him, I knew he was beside me as certainly as I know you are here, my dear."

Mom's face became rosy; she lifted her arms heavenward and in a voice, reverent with awe, she said, "And he is here now." In that hallowed moment we were overcome with the Lord's love and his mercy, as confirmed in Matthew 28:20, *"Lo, I am with you always"* (NASB). The exquisite comfort of that promise gave us the absolute assurance that we were never alone.

A year later my dad called us to hurry to Houston to see Mom. My husband and I raced to arrange a plane trip and as we flew there I recalled the special weekends Mom and I had shared over the past two and a half years. Would they be no more? I could not face the possibility.

We gathered at Mom's bedside and after a few words to each of us, she slipped into a brief coma and then left us to be with her Lord. His hand had been on her throughout her illness and that same hand now reached out to welcome her into heaven.

We had prayed for Mom's physical healing but it had not been granted. Other miracles, though, gave evidence of the Lord's power and grace. Mom had been uncomfortable at times but never in the pain that often accompanies cancer. She was able to remain at home and those she loved had been with her. She had lived far longer than the doctors had predicted. Most importantly, the Lord had been her constant companion and his peace had given her continual comfort.

I longed to have Mom back but consolation came whenever I prayed, "Thank You, Father God, that Mom is with you." Assured of His faithfulness, not only to my mother, but to me, I sensed an incredible joy in the midst of overwhelming sadness.

At the reception following the funeral, one of the elders who had anointed Mom with oil, confessed to me his faith had been shaken by Mom's death. I admitted I, too, had struggled as to why the Lord had denied our prayer for her healing.

I took his hand. "But I have realized our prayers were answered."

His brow furrowed. "I don't understand."

"We asked for Mom's health to be restored. It has been. Mom is alive and in perfect health. She's living joyously in Heaven with her Lord."

He nodded slowly and his face cleared. "You're right."

I smiled. "I have experienced a taste of that joy myself. It has come to me at the time of my greatest sadness."

Confess your faults one to another, and pray one for another,
that ye may be healed.
The effectual fervent prayer of a righteous man availeth much.

James 5:16 KJV

37

Once Upon a Cold Hot Water Day

Sherri Stewart

Do you know 1 Corinthians 1:27 where God chose the foolish things of the world to shame the wise? I am so glad God chose me as one of His little fools.

It was colder than most January days in Calgary, Alberta — so cold that I was reluctant to drive my old Volvo too far from home, but I hated to miss the first day of class at the university.

After dropping my son off at the babysitter's, I decided to take the subway, something I had never done before. A small voice inside reminded me that whenever I did something for the first time, I made mistakes — it's good that I wasn't studying to be a surgeon, right? But how hard could taking the subway be?

I bought my ticket but knew I would have to transfer downtown to another train that would take me to the university. I wasn't sure how to do that, but surely, someone would help.

When I arrived downtown, I jumped off the train and was waiting for the corresponding one to arrive when a thought struck me. A pot of potpourri was simmering on the stove at home. Great. Two hours had passed. Soon the water would evaporate, the pot would catch on fire, and we'd lose everything. I thought of my poor dog and decided to call a neighbor who had a key to my house. That's when I realized my purse was missing. I had left it on the train.

God help me.

Spying a pay phone, I took a deep breath, dug in my pockets for change and found some. My next-door neighbor wasn't home, but my husband was in town, which was rare since he worked for a hockey team that was always on the road. Bobby was gracious as always and didn't reprimand me.

While I waited for him to pick me up, I stopped the conductor of an arriving train and told him about my purse. He said he would alert the other drivers to be on the lookout.

As Bobby and I raced toward our house, I looked for rising smoke in the northeast. Bobby reminded me that we would have to cancel our credit cards and get a locksmith to unlock my car since we didn't have an extra key.

No smoke billowed out of the house, but I didn't wait for the car to slow down before I jumped out, opened the garage door, and ran into the kitchen. The red light on the stove was still on, the burner under the small pot was red hot, but the potpourri floating inside the pot wasn't simmering. I dipped my finger in the brown liquid. It was ice cold.

Ice cold.

The same God who parted the Red Sea and made the sun stand still kept the liquid on a red-hot burner ice cold.

But that's not all. A few hours after I had cancelled my credit cards, I received a call from the transit company. They had found my purse in a plastic bag. Someone had taken the cash but had left everything else — my passport and visa, my checkbook, credit cards, keys, and driver's license. I called the bank to see if they would disregard my request to cancel my cards but knew it was a lost cause. The woman at the bank said that the system had gone down after I called so my credit cards were still good.

I made a lot of mistakes on that cold January day, but God didn't reprimand me. I was doing enough of that myself. He made simmering water cold and made the bank's system stand still for a few hours — for me.

38

Consuming Hopelessness

Gayle Fraser

Now a word was brought to me stealthily
and my ear received a Whisper of it.
Job 4:12 NASB

The day had started out as a bad hair day. My hands, arms, shoulders and head hurt. With my fibromyalgia in full swing, nothing relieved my aching body.

Now I was pushing a shopping cart full of groceries uphill to the car. It is so hard to handle a cart when my arms hurt. I have to lift each heavy bag from the shopping cart into the car. At home, I have to carry each bag from the car to the kitchen and put away the groceries.

I felt sorry for myself.

As I lifted a bag into the car trunk, I noticed a grocery stock boy pushing a cart full of groceries as a man in a wheelchair followed close behind. As I lifted the second bag into my car, I thought, *at least he has help.*

When I turned to pick up my third bag of groceries, I heard the man in the wheelchair say to the box boy, "I don't need any further help loading the groceries into my van. I can finish things from here." The boy left.

He doesn't need any help? I questioned to myself. Come over here and help me.

I've got to watch this!

With care he lifted one bag full of groceries from the cart to his lap. With the use of his hands and arms, he moved the wheels of his chair to the side of his van, maneuvered a little to the right, backed up a little to the left, adjusted his chair until he was in just the right position to place the groceries in his van. He lifted the bag and placed it on the floor. Bag after bag, at least seven of them, with patience he continued until his cart was empty. He used one hand to guide his chair wheels and the other hand to push the empty cart into the holding rack.

He returned to the van, and with the strength of his arms and shoulders boosted himself to the floor of his vehicle. He then tugged his heavy chair into the van and pulled the door closed from the inside.

I thought about the process he would go through upon returning home. Using the strength of his arms, back and shoulders, he would lower the wheelchair from the van to the ground and unfold it. Then he would have to lower himself from his van into the wheelchair. He would then lift a heavy grocery bag and place it on his lap, roll the wheelchair up a ramp, open the door of his home and roll to the kitchen or dining area where he would drop off his groceries.

He would have to do that six more times. The patience and challenge of obtaining and disseminating the groceries amazed me. How did he unload the groceries from the bags to the storage area? Would he set two or three cans at a time on his lap? This process probably took him the rest of the day.

The man in the wheelchair had apparently found acceptance in his handicap. He didn't want anyone doing for him what he could do for himself, no matter how difficult, painful or how long it took.

I couldn't say that and I was ashamed.

Just when I was about to succumb to consuming hopelessness, that man taught me that self-pity was not pretty on me.

I felt so small. My Lord whispered, "Give thanks for the use of your hands, arms and legs."

I did, and also thanked God for the lesson taught by that man. I do not want to be a victim of hopelessness, but I want to be like that man — a brave survivor.

39

Why, God?

Larry C. Hoover
as told to Helen Hoover

God, I don't understand why you would allow my son to die? I've heard stories of when you kept a person from committing suicide. Why didn't you do that for Gary?"

It had been two years since the death of my son. I missed him greatly, but more than that I grappled with why God would allow it. Gary was only twenty-three, in good health, had a darling daughter and a good future ahead of him. Why didn't God intervene?

God is a good God, loving, faithful, forgiving, kind, and guides us. Allowing my son to die didn't seem to fit with the description of God that I knew was true.

As the days and weeks rolled by, I had not received any answer from God. Yet I knew God answered prayer and I had benefitted from his help in times past. Why wouldn't God answer me now?

The questioning of God consumed me and I was depressed, but I actually didn't care. I still had a loving wife who was concerned about me. I was glad our two other children were alive and well, but the why questions about Gary abounded. Even with the depression I had managed to continue working, but nothing else mattered much.

It was a ten-mile drive to my work place. In those twenty minutes, I normally complained to God about why he hadn't helped our son. One morning, I asked again "God, why didn't you prevent Gary from killing himself?"

I didn't hear an audible voice, but inside I knew God said, "Do you know why you want to know?"

"Hmm, well God since you asked, I guess I don't."

Immediately God came back with, "You want to know so that

you can judge my actions concerning Gary."

Uh oh, I suddenly realized that God was right. Now repentance on my part was in order. "God, I'm so sorry. I know that I have no right to judge you and your actions, please forgive me. Instead, I choose to trust you that what you did concerning my son was right and good."

That short discussion with God changed my outlook concerning God and Gary's death. The depression lifted and I began to look forward to living again. I realize I won't know, in this life, why God didn't change the outcome of Gary's decision, and the answer probably won't matter in my future life.

Over twenty years later, I still miss Gary, but I now enjoy my life. It is filled with activities, vacations, visits with family and friends. I continue to learn more about God through scripture, sermons and Bible studies.

God is a good God, even when I don't understand his actions.

40

Faith Is . . . ?

Annmarie B. Tait

"Faith is a Divine virtue by which we firmly believe the truths which God has revealed."

Ernie, Dee, Patty, or any of my other school friends who attended Holy Cross Grade School with me in the sixties know that this sentence is printed in the Baltimore Catechism as the one and only response to the question, "What is faith?" If you were in my class, you'd better know the answer or there would be no marching down the center aisle of church to receive the Sacrament of Confirmation from Cardinal Krol and that's all there was to it. Boiled down it meant, "Believing without proof."

In grade school, the lion's share of what I studied about our faith focused on learning the prayers, customs, traditions, and ceremonies of Catholicism. The study of it still captures my interest. Preparing to receive the sacraments of Penance, the Holy Eucharist, and Confirmation were high on the grade school list of religious priorities and we studied ardently for each. Still, for years the text book response to the question, "What is faith?" bewildered me just as much as when I was ten years old and memorized the answer for the sole purpose of getting through Confirmation class. I really didn't have a clue. To me it was just words on a page.

"Faith is believing without seeing." I heard that sentence repeated hundreds of times throughout the twelve years of my Catholic education, but mostly it was the fear of being cast into the "fires of Hell" that prompted me to profess my belief. The fires of Hell licked at my heels frequently for I was head of the class at rebelling against the rules . . . and Catholicism has an abundance of them. While still in grade school I vowed that if rebellion pointed me towards the fires of Hell, getting there was going to be a lot more fun than just being denied access to the pearly gates on a simple "she didn't believe without seeing" rap.

In high school I confused faith with hope. I often had faith that if I prayed hard enough for an A on my biology test, God in all His divine mercy would come through with an A for me whether or not I studied for the test. Those were the woeful days of a strained and often snubbed sense of faith. I mean, if I didn't get an unearned A by virtue of my strong faith, what the heck is the point?

Still, I muddled through high school, earning my A's rather than waiting for my faith to deliver them. In the meantime, I met my best friend every Sunday and we'd sit in the back of the church and giggle all the way through Mass whispering about boys, and school, and boys, and TV, and boys and boys and . . . boys. Rarely did we devote one single thought to the Faith. Frankly, I'm a little surprised we were not reprimanded for our behavior. We certainly deserved it.

As I grew older and life's challenges met me head on, I'd put one foot in front of the other and forge through each set of circumstances as best I could. I don't remember thinking much about faith and I rarely prayed for a miracle no matter what the situation. Not because I didn't believe in the possibility of miracles, but I figured my problems, no matter how great they were to me, had to register fairly low on God's priority list compared to all the war, crime, and famine on the planet.

By the time I was fifty-nine years old, faith had settled into my heart, and I take great comfort in it. Somewhere along the line I have turned into a believer of things for which I have no proof. I have faith that God sent his Son to die on the cross for the sins of mankind. I believe that Jesus would have died to save me even if I were the only person on the planet. I am that special and that loved as a child of God. I believe there is life after death and though I don't fully understand the concept of Heaven, I still believe that the kind and merciful God, whom I have loved in my own way all my life, will see me in His presence united with all those I love who have already departed this world.

The roots of my strong faith reach back to the Sisters of St. Joseph and the recitation of answers from the Baltimore Catechism. Not by virtue of memorizing, but rather by being exposed to their kindness, enthusiasm and dedication to us, all to honor the good God who gives us life, and because they believed without seeing.

Watching my mother and dad accept whatever joy or hardship they faced with gratitude and belief (without seeing) slowly pulled me into the cradle of faith that is now my anchor in life.

When the doctor explained to my mother that she was very near the end of her life and probably would not live longer than a few days, she took my hand. Then she squeezed it and looked into my eyes and said, "Listen to me, first you love God and you believe. After that everything works to the good."

I wish I could say that my faith has reached that depth. It has not yet, but it does grow stronger every day. And on days when it needs a boost I remember the sincerity in my mother's eyes in those last few moments of a lucid conversation with her. Sometimes I repeat her words in my head: "First you love God, and you believe. After that everything works to the good." My faith in this statement grows ever stronger.

Even though I never searched for it, somehow Faith found me.

What is faith?

It is the confident assurance that what we hope for is going to happen. It is evidence of things we cannot yet see (Hebrews 11:1 NLT).

41

Walk of Faith

Myrtle Thompson

I look to what the future holds with anticipation. It will not be in the realm of our world situation. That changes every day, and tomorrow is uncertain. But today I look back over my past with joy. It's as though I am looking down from the tip of K2, the famous mountain in the Himalayas. My husband and I could see its tip when we lived in Pakistan.

I remember the Persian New Year celebration, the Vernal Equinox, and the Jewish history of Iran where I taught in an International School. Emotionally, I feel the warm sand brushing my flip-flops as I walked across the desert in the UAE.

My life took on changes when I chose to follow Christ. For my 90th birthday celebration my pastor-son and his wife had a display table recounting my ten decades of change, from 1920 to the present. I have had the joy of seventy-four years given to God for His will.

I did not know what He had planned for me when I began this walk of faith. I had the *King James Version* of the Bible to guide my path. I read about God's promises to King David, such as Psalm 32:8: *"I will instruct thee and teach thee in the way which thou shalt go. I will guide thee with my eye."* I laid claim to the promises, believing them mine because they express the character of God and his child. I am one of his children by faith in Christ.

God's words in Jeremiah 29:11 about His people Israel says, *"I know the thoughts I think toward you, thoughts of peace and not of evil to give you an expected end."* I dared to believe I could trust God. I was a self-willed child who became His captive, wanting to be obedient to his calling. The NASV translates this verse, *"I know the plans I have for you" declares the Lord, "plans for welfare and not calamity to give you a future and a hope."* The *NIV Student Bible's* translation says, *"plans to prosper you and not harm you."*

Both are true and good, but had I read that translation in my early years, it might have left me thinking of material prosperity, maybe even worldly goods. I am thankful I have had no great excess, but always had enough.

A blind man has to depend on a guide. So it was with my faith in Christ. I often had to wait for light. My Shepherd has led me in paths not unlike those he set as a pattern when he trod the earth. When sheep follow the shepherd, they will travel uphill and down, experience the thorns of the bushes, the cuts in their feet, the desire for a cool drink, and the need for rest. They must learn to trust the shepherd. My Shepherd, who came from Heaven's glory, walked in paths of rejection while He was on earth. He was misunderstood. In human form, He faced some terrible tragic moments. One of His last promises was, "*I will not leave you comfortless, I will come to you.*" He is willing to walk beside us.

Several years ago I had a small circle of earth in my front lawn with a clematis vine in the center, surrounded by tulips. It could not withstand the stormy winds and was often blown over. I decided to get rid of the circle. I dug up the vine and replanted the bulbs. I thought I had gotten all of them, but each year a few tulip leaves would appear and be cut by the mower. We had an early spring this year. Two leaves popped out. They had struggled to stay alive, but were unable to grow and bloom. Deciding to give them a new chance to grow and bloom, I dug them out and replanted them.

That incident tells my story. There is never a victory without a struggle. My Christian life has sometimes been blown over by a strong wind and I was momentarily cut down. It was then God took me out of the darkness of earth where I was not able to grow as He planned.

God replanted me so I could bloom for his glory. For that, I give Him praise.

42

Storms of Life

Robert Cook

Advancement Through Adversity

Webster defines adversity as difficulties, misfortune, hardship, distress, disaster, suffering, affliction, sorrow, misery, tribulation, woe, pain, trauma. Whether it's in a novel, a movie, or life — overcoming adversity makes advancement happen.

Viewer Not Victim

We love it when people like us are challenged with insurmountable odds, overcome them, and become someone greater than they ever dreamed. We simply cannot get enough . . . until we are faced with trials ourselves. Then we want to crawl under a rock and throw ourselves a pity party. We forget there is something to gain from adversity — the triumphs and the transformation from mediocre to greatness. We might want to throw in the towel, blame God and walk away, convinced our life was better before we put our trust in Jesus.

We Question Everything

Why is this happening? I go to church. I pray. I read my Bible. Why is God doing this to me?

These are the wrong questions. We need to ask, what does God want me to learn from this? How is God developing my character through this trial? How is God strengthening my faith through this ordeal? How will God use this situation for His Glory?

In the Storm

Let's look at an example of how God used a potentially bad situation to strengthen his followers' faith and glorify God: *As evening came, Jesus said to his disciples, "Let's cross to the other side of the lake." He was already in the boat, so they started out . . . soon a fierce storm arose. High waves began to break into the boat until it was nearly full of water. Jesus was sleeping at the back of the boat with his head on a cushion. Frantically they woke him up, shouting, "Teacher, don't you even care that we are going to drown?" When he woke up he rebuked the wind and said to the water, "Quiet down!" Suddenly the wind stopped and there was a great calm. He asked them, "Why are you so afraid. Do you still not have faith in me?" And they were so filled with awe and said among themselves, "Who is this man, that event he wind and waves obey him?"* (Mark 4:35-41 NLT)

Don't Lose Faith

The disciples had witnessed Jesus perform many miracles, but in a moment of trouble, they forgot the power of Jesus. When we face the storms of life, it might seem like Jesus is sleeping and we are drowning in our troubles. We may have witnessed the power of Christ, but faced with a new adversity, we may forget those times of deliverance. In fear, we doubt Jesus' ability to see us through. But, if not for the storm, the disciples would not have witnessed the power of Jesus. Their faith grew that day.

Remember

The next time you face tough times, don't fall prey to fear and doubt. Go to the Lord and ask him to calm the storm and show you what he wants you to learn from it.

Like the hero in our favorite movie or book, we can grow through the conflict and adversity we face. Remember, when we are in the storm, Jesus is in the boat with us.

43

Losing to Gain

Anne Edwards

"If you try to keep your life for yourself, you will lose it. But if you give up your life for me, you will find true life."

~ Jesus (Matthew 16:25 NLT)

Ten years ago I was feeling lost, lonely, scared and hungry. While visiting Swannanoa Christian Ministries' lunch table at a Methodist Church, a woman told me about the Queen for a Day event that would take place at a Baptist church. She thought I might like to attend.

I had nothing to lose . . . and a whole lot to gain.

I grew up with parents who tried to shelter me. I had epilepsy and, in early years, wasn't allowed to be exposed to those who might hurt me. But as I grew older, I was a bit headstrong and, unfortunately, made many wrong decisions along the way.

At age twenty-two, my biggest mistake was the man I married. The best thing was, we had a daughter. He was abusive to me during the seventeen-and-a-half years we were married, and he raped our daughter. I learned later that he told her he would kill me if she told me.

When she was fourteen, she told someone she trusted. My husband was arrested and sentenced to jail. I got a divorce but my daughter was taken from me when a court decided that I was not capable of living on my own and raising a child.

Back then many people told me that I could never make it on my own, and I believed it. Now, I am blessed to know better. Especially meaningful to me is Psalm 139 that tells about God knowing me, loving me, and having a plan for my life. If only I had trusted his love back then.

He has always cared for us and promised never to leave us. We are the ones who leave Him or just never bother to know Him. Big Mistake! If only we would come to God and let Him do the leading, we would not have to hurt so much.

But I did not begin to find God's way until I attended Queen for a Day. I believe God led me there because the members made me feel loved and not judged. Later, I attended that church on Easter Sunday and gave my heart and life to Jesus Christ.

I was baptized along with another believer and we have grown together as sisters in Christ, forming a bond as strong as biological sisters, and we now serve our Lord. What a blessing to have a church family to love and support each other!

Don't think that becoming a Christian keeps trouble away. God often uses suffering and troubles to help us grow stronger. The Bible tells us that troubles help us learn to endure. Endurance develops strength of character.

I have been privileged to give my testimony at Queen for a Day gathering. What a joy to look out at tables decorated with the finest place settings a church member has and the creative centerpiece made or selected for each table, representing something special. The attendees come from many places, including homeless shelters and homes for abused women. These women are treated like queens. Men from the church, wearing white shirts, black pants, and aprons, show respect and serve their plates.

I tell them my story, just as I've heard other women's stories. I let them know that I've been blessed in so many ways since the Lord came into my life. I tell them they, too, can share in His blessings. They just have to admit their need for Him and give him their heart. Jesus said when he walked the earth: *"I am the way, the truth, and the life. No one can come to the Father except through me"* (John 14:6 NLT).

Scripture tells us that all have sinned, but if we confess that Jesus is Lord, and believe in our hearts that God raised him from the dead, we will be saved.

After the dinner, some of the women are given haircuts and styling by volunteers. They may go to the clothes closet for clothing, and receive bags of personal items.

They have been treated royally, like a Queen for a Day. They have discovered, as I did, that because our Father in heaven is the King of Glory, they may become a Princess forever.

44

What? Forgive Billy the Bully?

Robin Bayne

I won't date a guy who fights," I told Jim, my teenage friend. Occasionally, he picked fights. Once I'd glimpsed him in a boxing stance and flashed back to my childhood, when I'd been bullied. I recalled in vivid detail walking home from school with a smirking red-haired boy, Billy, walking backward in front of me with his fists in my face.

My parents had discussions with his parents, but they scoffed, insisting he was just being a boy. Anxiety often gripped me, since he lived in the house directly behind ours.

"I used to be pathetic because of a bully," I told Jim. "It's not something I can deal with in a boyfriend."

"I'm sorry," Jim said. "If it's that important to you, I'll work on it."

"Thank you." I gave him a big smile. "Now let's go for a drive where I grew up."

Jim nodded, and I looked from house to house as we drove. As we neared Billy the Bully's house, I saw a cluster of people in the front yard.

"Slow down." I said, then plastered my finger to the window. "That's him."

"Who?"

"Billy and his parents. They must still live there."

The car slowed and my gaze settled on Billy. I'd recognize that bright hair and freckled face anywhere. His ears stuck out like handles. He hadn't changed a bit.

"Should I stop and punch his lights out?" Jim asked.

"No!"

"Just checking. You want me to tell him off? You know, he could never get a girl as pretty as you. That should make you feel good."

My pulse pounded and I felt perspiration trickle down my sides. Jim was wrong — I didn't feel good. In fact, the longer I looked at Billy, the worse I felt.

For him.

Like the Grinch's heart on Christmas morning, mine expanded and I felt bad for the guy and hoped he had found, or would find, someone to love him. We're supposed to treat others as we want to be treated — and I didn't want any revenge for the past.

I decided to pray for Billy.

"So what do we do?" Jim asked.

"Let's just go," I said, and glanced at Billy one more time. He stood cross-armed watching us drive away. He didn't seem to have recognized me. But it didn't matter.

"I don't think these memories are going to bother me anymore," I said. It was time to leave my old neighborhood behind and forgive. I sent up my prayers, for me, and for Billy the Bully.

Never pay back evil for evil to anyone.
Do things in such a way that everyone can see you are honorable.

Romans 12:17 NLT

45

Through the Dark Days

Andrea Merrell

The phone rang late one evening, and every muscle in my body tensed. Was it one of my children? Another prank call? Maybe this time it was the police, the hospital, or — worse yet — the morgue.

With a shaky hand, I eased the phone to my ear. A raspy female voice said, "I know where your daughter is . . . almost OD'd."

My mind tried to shut out the words. It was hard to breathe. "Who is this?"

"Doesn't matter. Wanna know where she is or not? Her *friends* said if she died, they'd throw her in a dumpster and not think another thing about it."

This phone call came after years of dealing with my son's and daughter's addictions to drugs and alcohol. During those years, I struggled to trust God and hold fast to His promises as one day morphed into another, and things only got worse. I cried myself to sleep at night, cringed with fear every time the phone rang, and watched my children run from everything they had been taught.

Having a prodigal is devastating when you feel you've done all the *right* things — taking them to church, praying for them, and raising them in a godly environment. My kids went to Sunday school, VBS, and Christian camps. They never listened to secular music or read secular books. They could quote Scripture and knew all the popular Christian songs. Born again and baptized at an early age, they were good, upstanding, obedient kids. What could have possibly gone wrong?

The truth is: Even *good* kids rebel, and even *good* parents can end up with a prodigal . . . or in my case, two.

Raising teenagers is never easy, but it's hard to go to bed at night wondering when and *if* your children are coming home. I wanted to give up and stop praying. Stop caring. But God wouldn't let me. My mother-heart was shattered, and I wanted my family back.

God, how can this be? I prayed. *What more could we have done? Where are you?*

Friends told me not to worry. They assured me God would turn things around. *Easy for them to say*, I reasoned. *They've never been through this.*

My prayers continued, asking God for a sign — something to hold on to.

The answer finally came during a church service. My pastor asked those dealing with a rebellious child to come to the front. When I stepped forward, there was a surprised look on his face. I had been the church secretary for years, and he was unaware of my situation. Whether from pride or embarrassment, my husband and I had never confided in him and asked for help. We tried to carry the burden alone.

We had a visiting speaker that night. The speaker's wife wrapped her arms around me and prayed for my family. I don't remember a single word she said, but a tremendous weight lifted from me. For the first time since my nightmare began, there was no doubt God had heard my prayers.

There was no instantaneous miracle — at least not one that could be seen. My children didn't come home that night, the next, or the next. The miracle took place in me as God drew me closer than ever before. My peace and joy returned. My prayers were different. Each time I lifted my children up to the Lord, He seemed to orchestrate my prayers, assuring me He would save my children and bring them home.

The breakthrough came when my son approached his dad. He was miserable and looking for a way out. With strength only God can give, my son made a choice. He turned his back on the life he had been living, surrendered himself to God, and was miraculously delivered from drugs and alcohol. My hope was renewed. I believed it was only a matter of time before my baby girl would follow.

The night I received the phone call about my daughter was her wake-up call. When she returned home the next day, she had hit bottom. Three days later, she boarded a plane to Arizona to stay with her former youth pastor. Literally skin and bones, her face pasty white, her eyes dark and lifeless, she looked like "walking death." My heart broke watching her walk away, but God whispered His assurance that she was in His hands

Seven weeks later I flew to Arizona to pick her up. The young woman who met me at the airport was not the one I had sent away. She had gained weight, her skin was glowing, and her eyes radiated the love and life of Christ. She had been transformed from the inside out.

That was over twenty years ago. Both my children are now married with children of their own. A few years ago, my son gave his testimony to the students at summer camp. Knowing that many of his friends spent time in jail or are still living that lifestyle, reminds me to be thankful for God's love and faithfulness.

My daughter loves the Lord and desires to help others going through what she has faced and conquered. She is now one of my closest friends. Her life could have been snuffed out prematurely that horrible day we got the phone call. If she had ended up in a dumpster, we may never have known what happened to her. But God had other plans.

Through those dark days, I learned that God is loving and faithful, His Word is true, and prayer works. He also taught me to never, ever give up — no matter how impossible the situation may seem. Through prayer, God brought my prodigals home. He also brought me back to a place of rest that had been stolen by fear and worry.

God is a God of miracles and extraordinary answers to prayer. My children are living proof.

46
The Three Cs

Frank Stern

The gurney squeaked as they wheeled me from the Cardiac Intensive Care Unit to a regular hospital room. The surgeon had cracked open my chest and reamed three of four occluded arteries. A snake now twisted its way from my sternum to my belly button.

"I'm Sophia. I'll be your nurse today."

Her olive skin glistened. When she smiled, her nose crinkled. I learned later her family had immigrated to escape the civil war in Syria.

"You seem to be recovering nicely, Dr. Stern. Your vitals are excellent."

The bandage around my chest was gone. Several beeping devices had vanished from my monitor stand. For the first time in three days, I could move my arms and legs at will.

"We encourage you to get as much exercise as you're able. If you can get out of bed by yourself, do so. If you can go to the bathroom on your own, do so. Urinate into the pitcher and leave it on the sink in the restroom. Defecate into the toilet, but don't flush. I need to examine your stool before I flush it."

"I need to go right now," I said.

She disconnected my monitors and helped me to my feet. I felt a little wobbly and held her outstretched hand. Pulling the metal stand behind me, she escorted me into the bathroom.

"Will you be okay if I leave you?"

I nodded, she left, and I fainted.

Sophia helped me back to bed. I was lucky. I hadn't banged my head or ripped open stitches.

It was not the best time for me to be away. I kept thinking about situations I believed needed my help.

My daughter and son-in-law were experiencing significant problems in their marriage.

My granddaughter was failing in school.

I'd been a widower for four years. With the encouragement of my son and daughter, I had started dating. My son and my girlfriend fought.

Tom, a dear friend, came to visit. I shared my fears and apprehensions. It felt good to talk with someone who cared.

At the close of his visit, he asked if he could anoint me. I agreed.

From his briefcase, Tom took out an embroidered pouch and prepared the anointing oil. He said a few prayers, poured oil onto a white cloth, and anointed my forehead, heart and hands.

Afterwards, he recited the section from Deuteronomy, beginning "You shall love the Lord your God with all your heart, with all your soul and with all your might . . ." and sought God's blessing for me.

My friend Al, a Catholic priest, visited me next. Again I unburdened myself, sharing concerns about my heart, my health and my family. Al's a good listener. I felt better talking to him.

At the close of his visit, he pulled a black pouch from his cassock. "I brought you a rosary bead necklace and cross of polished olive wood made in Jerusalem, and I asked the bishop to bless it. I figured something from the Holy Land and a bishop's blessing might help. May I give it to you and say a prayer before I go?"

"I'm touched," I said.

The wooden cross and the prayer beads glistened under the electric lights. I was moved by the simplicity of his gift and by its intense spiritual qualities. "I'll treasure it. Thank you."

He asked God to heal both my body and soul. We hugged, and he departed.

It may have been my friends' visits, or my worries about my family, or the constant entrances and exits of the hospital staff, but I didn't sleep well that night. My chest hurt, my dreams disturbed me; I woke up sweating.

Next morning I had a third visitor, my friend Don, vice-principal of a local high school. As a teenager, Don's son had lived on the streets, hooked on methamphetamine. He died at twenty-five.

"Let me share one of the alphabet lessons I learned at Al-Anon," Don said after I revealed some of my worries. "Here are three C's I remind myself of every day: I didn't Cause the problem; I can't Control the problem; I can't Cure it."

After he left, I thought about the three C's. No matter which member of my family I focused on, the three C's applied. I didn't cause, I couldn't control and I couldn't cure my daughter's marital problems, my granddaughter's school problems, or my son's antipathy toward my girlfriend. All I could do was worry, and worrying accomplished nothing.

I never blame God when things go wrong. I believe God gave me the gift of life and the capacities to overcome its challenges.

The rest was up to me. God wasn't going to remedy my mistakes. But trying to do the right thing was a burden. When I missed the mark, I felt sad. When I hurt someone, I felt guilty. When I didn't know what to do, I felt inadequate.

One day, weary and downhearted, I gave it all to God.

"God, I'm failing. I can't make it on my own. I need help. Your help. I don't know where to go or what to do, so I'm leaving it up to you. I'm putting myself in your hands. Tell me what you want me to do. Please."

Tears streamed down my cheeks.

I decided to stop worrying about situations out of my control. I resolved to let those with the problems search for solutions. I gave up feeling guilty about mistakes I made two or three decades ago.

A weight lifted from my chest.

Energy and hope flooded my body.

Two years have passed. I play tennis, dine with friends, work. God has blessed my life, and I'm grateful.

I realize now how special my friends are and tell them so frequently.

I spend time with my children and grandchildren, declaring

constantly how much I love them. But I let them solve their own problems.

I enjoy the weather more, the smile of strangers, and the greetings of neighbors and passers-by. I give more easily to charities, do more random acts of kindness, and work harder to feed the hungry and shelter the homeless.

I guess this is what God wants me to do.

I expected lightning and thunder, a heavenly voice booming in my head, a divine decree that made my body quake and my mind tremble. I didn't receive any of those.

Nonetheless, my life changed significantly once I gave myself up to God. I'm happier now. More patient, more loving and more fulfilled.

47

Love Transcends Grief

Helen L. Hoover

Our family and friends gathered at the hospital while we waited for the results of medical tests performed on our twenty-three-year-old son, Gary. Due to depression, bad decisions, and loss of a job, Gary had shot himself the night before.

"I'm sorry, your son is brain dead," the neurosurgeon reported.

Hope evaporated. Grief dropped on us like a heavy rock. Shame permeated our soul. Unending questions surfaced about God's goodness, our son's decisions, and our own inability to prevent this. "Why? Why?" This became a recurring question for months. An unwanted journey started for my husband Larry and me.

The minutes slowly turned into hours, and hours into days. Decisions had to be made that we didn't want to make: what organs to donate, funeral arrangements, disposing of his belongings, and selling his house. We were not prepared for this unexpected journey.

The funeral arrived. We were flooded with condolences, food, and flowers from wonderful friends and extended family. We appreciated their help and company, but a hole had appeared in my heart. "God, how do I deal with the emptiness that Gary's death has produced?"

Our two other children and their spouses helped us pack and sort while we decided and agonized on what to do with his belongings. Should we give everything away, keep it all, separate it out, save special items? What are the right choices?

We had nothing in our background on which to base our decisions.

"Oh here's the black jacket that Gary looked so good in," our daughter Ginger said. "What do you want to do with his pictures?" asked our older son, Grant.

Soon our family went back to our normal routine, but life wasn't normal. Our fun-loving son wouldn't be showing up on our doorstep with his humorous renditions of life. We would need one less chair at the table for family celebrations.

The physical aspects of this journey were soon resolved, but the emotional part continued traveling with us. Tears rolled down our cheeks occasionally. Anger reared its head at times. Loneliness came in to hang around. Questions abounded.

Through all aspects of this grief journey, though, God walked with us. At the beginning we didn't recognize his presence, but in hindsight we realize his love stayed with us in a variety of ways.

"George talked with me again at lunch time," Larry reported when he arrived home from work.

"Johnna is going with me to the dentist tomorrow and then we'll have lunch," I said. "We'll have lots of time to chat."

"Read this note from Laura that arrived in the mail today." I told Larry. "She is recounting some delightful things about Gary."

The time that friends and extended family spent with us was invaluable to keep us progressing on this journey. The multitude of notes and letters that arrived kept reminding us of God's love and the senders' love.

"Look at this scripture," I told Larry as I handed him my Bible. I pointed out Romans 15:13: *"May the God of hope fill you with all joy and peace as you trust in him, so that you may overflow with hope by the power of the Holy Spirit"* (NIV).

I knew we were going to make it. God kept assuring us with His Word.

It's been over twenty years since we began our unwanted journey. God has continued to help, guide, comfort, and love us along the pathway. We still don't know the answers to our "Why?" questions, but we've resolved to trust God anyway.

Our journey started with unbelievable grief and then progressed into a greater understanding of God's love for us. We are thankful He never left us.

48

Disintegrating Shoes

Rebecca Carpenter

As I walked across the church foyer, I began limping. *What happened?* I looked behind me to see a trail of black. A large piece of black rubber lay on the pristine floor.

Standing like a flamingo, I pulled off one shoe. A gaping hole replaced the heel. The mess that marred the foyer came from me.

How would I be able to stand as a volunteer greeter for the special service with a broken shoe?

I hobbled to the information desk and relayed my pathetic story. The lady called the church's man-of-all-trades. Soon he appeared and assessed my damaged shoe.

"Glue won't help," he said.

"Could you tape it?" I asked.

"That's what I was thinking," he said.

With one shoe on and walking on my bare toes to keep my body even, I nonchalantly waddled into the volunteers' meeting room with my friend.

We stood in line for our dinner and laughed to ourselves. When we sat down, I told other diners at our table about my shoe problem.

Minutes later, my shoe repairer reappeared with my shoe. Black duct tape encircled the entire back of my shoe. I showed his handiwork to my friends and put it on.

After eating, we received instructions and assignments for the night. When I stood to join my group, something didn't feel right. I looked down. A pile of black surrounded my chair. The sole of the toe on the taped shoe dangled. With trepidation, I took off the second shoe and saw black powder fall from it.

To prevent making more messes, I took off both shoes and

started for the door to find my special repairman. Thankfully, he wasn't far away. When I held the pair of shoes in front of him, he smiled.

"I wondered if the other part would go too," he said and took my shoes.

Another volunteer in a wheelchair offered me her sandals, but they were three sizes too small. We laughed as I waited.

Time was getting close for our jobs to begin. While my shoes were missing, I pondered my options. I could hide and refuse to help out. Wear too-short shoes. Go barefooted and risk embarrassment and having my toes squashed by the hundreds of people entering the doors.

When my shoe repairman returned, I thanked him profusely for the unusual task. His kindness and servant's heart touched me. Even with unique shoes, I would be able to serve too.

Bits of upturned tape clung to my feet. But with a few adjustments, they worked.

I thought of our speaker for the night and knew I need not be embarrassed to serve our community even if I had no shoes.

Nick Vujicic, who was born without arms or legs, inspires millions with his story. He appeals to young and old as he shares the Good News of Jesus all over the world.

How appropriate that my shoes disintegrated just before he was to speak. He has one tiny foot with two small toes which he uses as fingers. That bare foot reminded me of mine. He has adapted to his condition and overcome depression. God uses him daily.

Perhaps my story about the disintegrating shoes will inspire others to accept difficult situations and go on. To not let inconveniences become monumental obstacles. God takes us through all sorts of situations and joins us there.

At one time in my life, I would have franticly tried to find a store and buy new shoes. Perhaps I would have even declined serving. However, losing my husband, parents, other family members and friends within a short time has given me a new perspective.

When I thought of Nick I really didn't care if I had to go without shoes. My situation was nothing compared to his. I might keep my crumbled, patched-up shoes as a special reminder, a perfect story of what is truly important.

49

Guess Who's Calling

Margaret Peterson

Sheila loved her new in-laws but they were far from God's Kingdom. The only time they spoke his name was when they were angry. And they were often angry . . . never with her, but frequently with each other. Her brother-in-law, Denny, had not spoken to his sister, Marion, in two years.

Sheila looked for opportunities to tell them of the Lord's love for them. She prayed daily for them, eyes closed behind her glasses and brunette head bent in reverence.

Winter came early to Wisconsin the year she married into Ray's family and she prayed for safety for her new relatives as they drove the icy country roads.

One evening Ray banged through the door with a frown on his face. "That stupid brother of mine was speeding and hit a patch of ice. He crashed his truck and ended up in the hospital." Ray ran a hand through his dark curls. "Grab your coat, Sheila, and let's go see how he is."

Denny had two cracked ribs and a broken wrist that would heal but his truck was beyond repair. Ray surveyed his brother's swollen face, with several open cuts and relief and anger mixed in his voice as he said, "You could have been killed, you idiot."

Sheila put her hand on Ray's shoulder and shook her head at her husband. "We're thankful you weren't more seriously hurt," she told Denny and smoothed his hair with her other hand. "I've prayed for your safety and the Lord protected you." Denny stared at her and then at his brother.

At Christmas Sheila invited the family to dinner and then to an evening service at church.

They all accepted the dinner invitation and they all made excuses to avoid attending the church service. Sheila was disappointed but it did not deter her from continuing to pray for their salvation.

The first week of the new year brought a heavy snowfall, and as usual, Sheila interceded for safety of the family and added a prayer for Denny who was home with a throat infection.

She stopped in with some homemade chicken soup and found him pale and trembling. "Oh, you're still really ill aren't you?"

He shook his head and croaked out, "No, it's not that."

"What's happened?"

"I . . . I went out to the shed about ten minutes ago to get some wood for the fireplace." He waved his hand toward the rear of the house. "And then . . . " He wiped his hand over his face.

"And then what?"

"I saw there was a lot of snow on the shed roof. I thought when I was feeling better I would get it off before . . . " He drew a shuddering breath. " . . . before the roof caved in." He closed his eyes. "I reached for some of the small logs and I heard the phone ring. So . . . so I went back to the house." Denny opened his eyes and stared into space.

"Go on."

"I couldn't believe it." He bit his lip. "It was Marion."

Sheila's eyes grew wide. "After all this time she called you?"

"Yeah."

"No wonder you seem a bit dazed."

"That's not why." Denny swallowed a couple of times. "While I was talking to her the shed roof fell in."

"What?"

"Yeah. The whole thing caved in. And, Sheila, big shards of glass from the window were stuck in the ground right by the woodpile where I'd been standing."

Sheila gasped. "You'd . . . you'd be dead if Marion hadn't called."

"I know," Denny said slowly.

"It's not as if she phones all the time is it?" Denny shook his head. Sheila grabbed his quivering hands. "This is the second time lately that God has protected you. He's really trying to show you that he's there for you."

"I think he is."

"I'm sure of it. He wants you to know that he loves you."

"You really think so?"

Sheila nodded and went on to tell him about God's plan of salvation; how God had sent Jesus to make a way to the Heavenly Father's Kingdom. Denny listened with tears glistening in his eyes.

That afternoon Denny became a brother, as well as a brother-in-law, to Sheila. He heard the call, joined the Father's family and became a son in God's Kingdom.

Sheila rushed home to share her joy with Ray.

"Marion called Denny?" Ray said. "That's amazing. Did he tell you what she said?"

"No, he was too shaken by the shed's collapse to elaborate." She unwound her scarf and unbuttoned her coat.

Ray took them to the closet. Sheila heard his muffled words, "Tell Marion."

"I encouraged Denny to tell her," Sheila said when Ray emerged from the closet. "And to share the miracle of his new faith with her."

Ray smiled. "Marion making the effort to call Denny could mean the beginning of all my family coming to the Lord."

Sheila nodded. "It's what I've been praying for."

"Me, too."

"Let's thank God for Denny's commitment and pray for his conversation with Marion," Sheila said and took Ray's hand. They went down together on their knees in the middle of the living room.

Three weeks later Sheila invited Ray's family for dinner to celebrate Ray's twenty-eighth birthday. His parents declined since they were leaving Wisconsin that weekend for a trip. But Denny and Marion accepted the invitation.

Sheila prepared a festive meal. The smell of roast wafted across the frosty air when she opened the door to greet Denny, who had arrived in his new truck. His eyes sparkled and his smile was wide. "Bless you, Sheila," he said as they walked into the living room. "Thanks for the Bible. I've been reading it a lot." He gave her a hearty hug. "My life feels newer than my truck."

They laughed together.

"What's the joke?" Ray said as he came up behind Sheila.

"No joke." Denny's voice boomed with enthusiasm. "I was just telling Sheila how much my life has changed since I became a Christian."

The doorbell jangled and Ray opened the door to his sister, Marion. In contrast to Denny, her smile was small and did not last. Her gray eyes held no light and in a low voice she said, "Happy Birthday, Ray."

"Hey, Sis, thanks. So good to have you join us."

Sheila stepped forward. "Yes, we're delighted you came." She hugged Marion. "Let me take your jacket."

Denny said, "I've got it." He assisted Marion as she shrugged out of her white parka. "It's great to see you again." His voice cracked with emotion. "The last time we were here was at Christmas and I was guilty of not speaking to you then."

Marion looked down.

"Didn't even wish you a Merry Christmas. What a jerk I was." He ran his hand over his face. "Will you forgive me?"

Marion nodded. Denny reached for her hands. "I love you." Marion's gaze lingered on the carpet.

The prolonged silence was broken by the oven timer's beep. "Oh, dinner's ready," Sheila said. "C'mon everyone, to the table."

Ray finished the last bite of his chocolate birthday cake and blew a kiss to his wife. "Darling, that meal was superb."

"It sure was," Denny said and grinned. He patted his stomach with a grin. "Thanks, Sheila, for all your work." Marion, who had said little during the dinner, expressed her thanks.

"I'm doing the dishes," Denny said and he began collecting plates.

"No, you're a guest," Sheila said but Denny chortled. "Nope, I'm your brother." He laughed and picked up another plate.

Marion stared at him. "You seem different than you used to be."

Denny put down the plates, the smile left his face and with a serious tone to his voice he said, "I am different. Like I told you on the phone, Marion, Jesus has changed my life."

"I don't understand." A frown wrinkled her brow. "How could that be possible?"

"Marion . . . " Sheila said but Ray shook his head and put his finger to his lips.

"Denny, why not leave the dishes for now and tell us your story?"

And Denny did.

Marion sat like a statue with her gaze riveted on him. He spoke with a fervent sincerity that brought tears to her eyes. They rolled unheeded down her pale cheeks and made small circles on her green slacks.

At the conclusion of Denny's story she said, "Could Jesus change my life like that?" She swiped at her tears. "It's such a mess."

Denny reached over and put his hand on his sister's shoulder. "He can do for you what he's done for me."

"And for me," Sheila said.

"And for me," Ray said.

Marion looked around the table at the three of them. "What do I have to do?"

"Ask Him to take over your life and make it His own," Denny said. He took one of his sister's hands and Ray took the other as Marion prayed the first prayer of her life.

The other three then joined in thanking the Father that Marion had called Denny, and now . . . God had called them both.

Jesus asked, *"Must I do miraculous signs and wonders before you people will believe in me?"* John 4:48 (Author's Paraphrase)

50

The Window of My Soul

Brenda Miller

Many seasons have come and gone during my seventy years, and I have always relished the changing of seasons. The state of Kentucky guarantees we will experience the wonder of four seasons, sometimes from one day to the next — sunburn one day, frostbite the next. As I write this, fall is swiftly overtaking the heat of summer, but to be honest, I am dreading the drab and gloomy days ahead.

Not only is the weather changing, but a new season of my life is beginning. A more challenging season as a widow also troubles me. It's been over three months since my husband, known as Tommy, or Grandad, now resides in his eternal home. Not since my college days have I lived alone. I question, "Why have I come to this hour so soon?" Yet, I am grateful for having had almost fifty years of marriage.

With a troubled mind, I question God's purpose for me. Why am I being hurled toward the wintertime blues with heaviness of heart, soul, and mind? I have to confess my temptation to shut the windows and doors and turn off the Light of my life. My responses to grief and pain from a hip replacement, two months after Tommy's death, are emotionally and physically bearing down hard.

In isolation I gaze out my sunroom's double window upon God's miraculous creation, and my thoughts gush out in a flood of tears. Aching for a revelation from the Spirit, I search the window of my soul for God to point me in his direction as I meditate on his Word, which says in Philippians 1:6, *"I am sure of this, that he who started a good work in you will carry it on to completion until the day of Christ Jesus"* (CSB).

Solitude can be refreshing if it is used as a time to meditate and reflect on positive thoughts, especially those from the Spirit. Jesus went off alone many times to be with his Father to pray. But, keep watch. Solitude can also be a time when the deceiver comes to tempt and torment because as Matthew 26:41b tells us, *"The spirit is willing, but the flesh is weak"* (CSB).

Satan tempts me with the thoughts that I am finished, I have no purpose, I am all alone, and nobody cares. Following the example of David, I open the Word of God and meditate on God's promises. Like Jesus, I rebuke the liar with Scripture. As I examine the window of my soul, I reflect on God's goodness and mercy in my life. I remember his promise to never leave me or forsake me, especially in my loneliness and grief. I meditate on Psalm 42:5: *"Why, my soul, are you so dejected? Why are you in such turmoil? Put your hope in God, for I will still praise him, my Savior and my God"* (CSB).

I hope for a new purpose, or a revival of purpose, as I continue to trust God my Father, and Jesus Christ my Savior, during this season and hour of my life.

There is a time for everything,
and a season for every activity under heaven.

Ecclesiastes 3:1 NIV

51

The Road Least Traveled

Dr. Jayce O'Neal

Two roads diverged in a yellow wood, I took the one less traveled by,
and that has made all the difference

~ Robert Frost

When I was seven years old I jumped off a high dive. It seemed to shock everyone in the pool that day, especially my mother. I don't know if you were like me or not, but when I was young I seemed willing to take more risks. I rode my bike off ramps. I didn't mind talking to new kids. However, it seems that the older I get, the more fearful I am of taking risks.

Fear is an active barrier to a Christian who wants to obey God, because at some point God will likely ask us to do something that might just freak us out. If fear is the barrier then comfort is the placebo of safety, but often it simply lulls us into disobedience.

For many, it is easy to lose that willingness to step out in faith, to take risks, to let go of our "security." The question I ask myself is, "Have I gotten too comfortable?"

I hear many Christians complain that America is slipping from its Christian roots, yet those same people seem unwilling to take any risk outside of posting their thoughts on social media.

When reading the Bible, it's easy to see that when God moved, it was rarely safe. Moses confronted Pharaoh, David took on a giant. The disciples left their jobs and families to follow Jesus.

Would we be so bold? If God spoke to us in a burning bush would we obey or suspect we were suffering from heat stroke? Would we confront a giant? Would we drop everything to follow Jesus?

Let's even consider small things. What if God asked us to stop drinking coffee, stay off the internet, walk more and drive less? Have we become too comfortable? Are we hearing God or is our caffeine, air conditioning, and favorite TV shows drowning out his voice? The truth is, that *most* of the time, *most* of us take the road *most* travelled, the path of least resistance and *most* comfortable.

I wonder what kind of impact Christians would make if we stopped complaining about what is wrong in the world and instead decide to truly obey God in every aspect of our lives. But to obey, means letting go of control. It requires faith. Hebrews 11:6 (ESV) tells us, *"Without faith it is impossible to please him."*

To be honest, in my weaker moments I'm not interested in what pleases God. I'd much rather he please myself by giving me what I want. I want to be comfortable. I fear, fear. Yet, God calls us to have faith.

What is the barrier to faith for you? Money? People? Regardless, of our barriers to obedience, we must remember the words of Jesus found in Luke 14:33 (ESV), *"Any one of you who does not renounce all that he has cannot be my disciple."*

Ouch. Is there something you find difficult to renounce? For me, it is control. I want to know what I'm doing and where I'm going, yet I know, when God asks me to do something, I won't always know how it will turn out.

When God moves, it is rarely safe, but it is always right. Moses helped deliver Israel, David became King, the disciples witnessed the life of Jesus. As difficult as it may seem, when we step out in faith to obey God, we can trust that His way is better than ours. Psalm 20:7 tells us *"some trust in chariots and some in horses, but we trust in the name of the Lord our God."* (ESV)

Let us not be deceived by comfort, let us be willing to make the dive when God asks, because most likely, the path he is asking you and me to travel is not the road most travelled.

. . . the gateway to life is small, and the road is narrow,
and only a few ever find it.
~ Jesus (Matthew 7:14 NLT)

52

The Waiting Room of Prayer

Norma C. Mezoe

I cried out to God in my sorrow,
"I can't bear this pain anymore.
Please take this heartache from me
and fling it from my door."

But God, in His all-knowing wisdom,
smiled and slowly shook His head,
and then, I was gently ushered
into God's waiting room instead.

If your prayers seem to be unanswered,
and you think God does not care,
you may find that you are resting
in the waiting room of prayer.

About the Authors

Robin Bayne is an award-winning author of more than 20 novels, novellas and short stories. She writes sweet and Christian romance, as well as devotionals. She compiled *Words to Write By,* a devotional collection for Christian writers. Robin lives in Maryland and works a day job in mortgage banking. Visit her at www.robinbayne.com.

Sheryl H. Boldt serves as a faith/church guest columnist for several newspapers including *The Tallahassee Democrat, The Tifton Gazette*, and *The Wakulla News.* Her goal is to honor God and encourage others to experience His loving presence in a life-changing way. Visit her blog, Today Can Be Different at (www.TodayCanBeDifferent.net).

Sherry Boykin is a storyteller, a chronic believer, and a recovering old maid. Her experiences in singlehood and marriage, inner-city & suburban ministries, and Peruvian Amazon and men's-dorm-living shape her life and compel her to share how God refuses to slacken His pursuit of us. She lives with her husband and daughter in northeast Pennsylvania. Find encouragement and more at SherryBoykin.org.

David Brannock is a writer who enjoys creating dramas for the screen and the stage. His screenplay *Unveiled* won first place for film scripts in the Foundations Award contest at the 2018 Blue Ridge Mountains Christian Writers Conference. David has also had two table graces published in *Guideposts.* He currently serves as a church lay speaker and a Word Weavers mentor. David and his family live in east Tennessee. Connect with him at DavidBrannock.com.

Dr. Timo Budarz is professor of physics at Liberty University in Virginia. He earned a Ph.D in theoretical physics from Purdue University. Besides scientific journal articles, his authoring includes an open-source, three-volume textbook for engineering physics, and multiple publications as an automobile journalist for both *DSport* and *Turbo* magazines. He enjoys traveling and spending time with his wife, two boys, baby daughter, bicycle racing, and playing finger-style guitar and improvisational piano. mailto:timobudarz@yahoo.com

Mirjam Budarz was born in Finland and lived many years in Germany. She now lives in beautiful coastal North Carolina. She loves spending time with her children and grandchildren. Two of her four children live in Europe, where she enjoys summer visits to them. She also loves Israel and is learning Hebrew. She has journaled for over half a century and written many short stories. A local newspaper published "Sharing Beauty" about gardening. "French Tutor Needed" appears in the Guidepost book, *Extraordinary Answers to Prayer.* """Uninvited Visitor" and the poem "Weathered Old House" are published in *Precious, Precocious Moments.* Mirjam also has done illustrations for two children's books. She writes nonfiction and fiction. mirjambudarz@yahoo.com

Rebecca Carpenter is a retired teacher who lives in Central Florida. As a member of WordWeavers International, she has won numerous awards for her devotionals. Her writings have been in *Clubhouse Magazine,* several local magazines and newspapers, as well as numerous *Moments* anthologies. After losing her husband and parents, she wrote a devotional book *Ambushed by Glory in My Grief.* Rebecca stays busy spending time with her granddaughters, going to lunch with friends, doing outreach projects, reading, and encouraging those who are grieving. racarp5050@hotmail.com

Robert Cook is the author of *Regener8* and *Illumin8* (teen devotionals), and *Youthanize: The Death of the Traditional Youth Ministry*. Robert ministers in Philadelphia, Pennsylvania with his wife Stephanie, son Christian, and several beloved pets. Find more about Rob on Facebook or at www.robcookunderground.com.

Lola Di Giulio De Maci is a retired teacher whose stories have appeared in numerous *Chicken Soup for the Soul* books, *The Los Angeles Times*, children's magazines and books, and columns written for several newspapers. She writes from her loft overlooking the San Bernardino Mountains.

Diana Derringer is an award-winning writer and author of *Beyond Bethlehem and Calvary: 12 Dramas for Christmas, Easter, and More!* Hundreds of her articles, devotions, dramas, planning guides, Bible studies, and poems appear in 40-plus publications, including *The Upper Room, The Christian Communicator, Clubhouse, Kentucky Monthly, Seek,* and *Missions Mosaic,* plus several anthologies. She also writes radio drama for Christ to the World Ministries. Her adventures as a social worker, adjunct professor, youth Sunday school teacher, and friendship family for international university students supply a constant flow of writing ideas. Visit her at dianaderringer.com. You can also find her on Facebook, Twitter, LinkedIn, Instagram, Goodreads, and Pinterest.

Anne Edwards is a volunteer for First Baptist Swannanoa and Swannanoa Christian ministries. She crochets scarves for Queen for a Day, a prison ministry, Operation Christmas Child, and crochets prayer blankets for the sick. Anne enjoys going on trips with seniors, and being with family making beautiful memories together. She prays for people who are going through hard times, hopes her story will let those with epilepsy know they are able to live a full life, and that God may bless each of you.

Ivette Ellis, aka Eve, is an aspiring harpist, psalmist, and creative writer. She is the author of *Whisper to Us: Hope for Change and Recovery*, a resource for those struggling with resentment and cyclical disobedience to Jehovah God. In the anthology, *Fifty Over 50: Who Is That Woman in The Mirror?* she details the early adulthood years of her life as she walked out her healing journey toward wholeness. Additionally, Eve received a first-place award for short nonfiction in the 2017 Georgia Peach Writer's Contest. She continues to write inspired articles and poetry, and plays simple harp instrumentals through her website Songbirdscribe.com.

Bobbie Ann DuPree Foshee is mother of two, grandmother of eight, and great-grandmother of seven. Bobbie has been married to her high school sweetheart for over fifty years. You may find her in your local library, courthouse, or cemetery in search of long-lost ancestors, an endeavor which led to her membership in the DAR and the DAC. In her spare time, she enjoys gardening, genealogy, and painting. Bobbie and her husband make their home in south Florida.

Gayle Fraser's writing focuses on Christian characteristics for young people. She has self-published scriptural guideline, *Grandma's Faithfulness*, for grandparents when praying for their grandchildren; a curriculum, *Shhh, I'm a Secret Sister,* for preteen girls promoting healthy Christlike lifestyles; a devotional, *Abba Whispers*; and Little Cab Press published her first children's book, *Our Home Sweet Home*. She has been published in *Chicken Soup for the Soul*; two of Yvonne Lehman's Moments anthologies, including *Moments With Billy Graham; Little Cab's Christmas Anthologies;*

and Memoir Stories for her grandchildren. She and her husband smuggled Bibles into China, participated in the Billy Graham's Crusade in Moscow, Russia, and toured Israel. Gayle is a member of Word Weavers International and lives in Arizona.

Phil Gladden writes a weekly newspaper column for the *Bourbon County Citizen* in Paris, Kentucky. "Phil's Philosophical Fodder" won third place at the Kentucky Press Association's Winter Editorial Convention in 2018. Phil has written an article to be included in the *Divine Moments'* 2019 Christmas book and has also begun to write poetry.

Lydia E. Harris has been married to her college sweetheart, Milt, for more than 50 years. She enjoys spending time with her family, which includes two married children and five grandchildren aged 8 to 19. She is the author of *Preparing My Heart for Grandparenting: For Grandparents at Any Stage of the Journey*. Her latest book is *In the Kitchen with Grandma: Stirring Up Tasty Memories Together*. With a master's degree in Home Economics, Lydia creates and tests recipes with her grandchildren for *Pockets* magazine and Focus on the Family's *Brio* and *Clubhouse* magazines. She also pens the column "A Cup of Tea with Lydia," which is published across the US and Canada. It's no wonder she's known as "Grandma Tea."

Jonathan Hayashi is a reformed Baptist, pastor theologian, Christian writer, and speaker. He currently serves as a pastoral staff at Troy First Baptist Church in Troy, Missouri. His love for the local church propels all he does, including his current pursuit of a Doctoral degree in Biblical Counseling at the Southern Baptist Theological Seminary in Louisville, Kentucky. He is the author of *Ordinary Radicals: A Return to Christ-Centered Discipleship*. You can follow Jonathan on Twitter @jonathanhayash or check out his personal blog, Evangelica Sola.

Judith Victoria Hensley is an award winning retired educator, newspaper columnist, author, and photographer. She considers herself a story gatherer and has completed many books comprised of inspirational stories from a variety of individuals. Her latest book *Warrior Women, Overcomers* is the fifth in the *Warrior Women* Series. She resides in the mountains of southeastern Kentucky and enjoys the beauty of God's handiwork in the region.

Helen L. Hoover and her husband are retired and live in Northwest Arkansas. Sewing, reading, knitting, traveling, and helping her husband with home repair occupy her time. Word Aflame Publishing, T*he Secret Place*, *Word Action Publication*, *The Quiet Hour*, T*he Lutheran Digest*, *Light and Life Communications*, *Chicken Soup for the Soul*, and *Victory in Grace* have published her devotionals and personal articles. Visits with their two living children, grand-children and great-grandchildren are treasured.

Alice Klies has written since she could hold a pencil. She is currently president of Northern Arizona Word Weavers. It is through their encouragement Alice began to submit her work for publication. She has nonfiction and fiction stories published in seventeen anthologies. She is a eight-time contributor to *Chicken Soup for the Soul* books and has articles published in *Angels On Earth, AARP* and *Wordsmith Journal.* She has also been featured in the *Women of Distinction* magazine. Little Cab Press released Alice's novel, *Pebbles in My Way*, a fiction based on her testimony, in September 2017. Besides her involvement in Word Weavers, she is a deaconess and Stephens Minister in her church. Alice serves on two non-profit boards: The Professional Women's Group and Sisterhood Connections LTD. Alice is a retired teacher who resides with her husband and two Golden Retrievers in beautiful Cottonwood, Arizona. She prays her stories give readers encouragement, laughter and maybe even tears.

Yvonne Lehman is compiler and editor of the *Divine Moments* series (*Moments with Billy Graham* is a Selah finalist), author of 59 novels and several non-fiction books. She was founder and director of the Blue Ridge Mountains Christian Writers Conference for 25 years and the Blue Ridge Novel Retreat for 12 years. She and Cindy Sproles now direct the Writing Right Mentoring Service for writers. Her recent release is a novella in T*he Reluctant Brides* collection. Her most popular novel is *Hearts that Survive—A Novel of the Titanic.*

Diana Leagh Matthews is a vocalist, speaker, writer, and genealogist. During the day, she is a certified Activities Director for a nursing facility. She is a Christian Communicators graduate. She has been published in several anthologies, including several *Moments* books. She currently resides in South Carolina. Visit her at www.DianaLeaghMatthews.com and www.alookthrutime.com.

Bennie McDonald is a deacon and Sunday school director at West Hall Baptist Church in Flowery Branch, Georgia, and a major in the Civil Air Patrol. He was formerly with the US Postal Service and the US Army. He studied professional photography at the University of North Georgia-Gainesville.

Beverly Hill McKinney has published over 300 inspirational articles in such publications as *Good Old Days, Breakthrough Intercessor, Just Between Us, Woman Alive, P31* and *Plus Magazine.* She has devotions in *Cup of Comfort Devotional Daily Reflections of God's Love and Grace, Open Windows, God Still Meets Needs* and *God Still Leads and Guides.* Her stories have been featured in anthologies such as *Christmas Miracles, Men of Honor,* Guidepost's *Extraordinary Answers to Prayer, Christian Miracles, Precious Precocious Moments, Additional Christmas Moment* and *Loving Moments.* She has also self-published two books, *Through the Parsonage Window* and *Whispers from God: Poems of Inspiration.* She graduated from the Jerry B. Jenkins Christian Writer's Guild and lives in Oregon.

Andrea Merrell is an associate editor with Christian Devotions Ministries and Lighthouse Publishing of the Carolinas. She is also a professional freelance editor and was a finalist for the 2016 Editor of the Year Award at Blue Ridge Mountains Christian Writers Conference. She teaches workshops at writers' conferences and has been published in numerous anthologies and online venues. Andrea is a graduate of Christian Communicators and a finalist in the 2015 USA Best Book Awards. She is the author of *Murder of a Manuscript* and *Praying for the Prodigal.* Her newest book, *Marriage: Make It or Break It,* is available on Amazon. For more information visit www.AndreaMerrell.com or www.TheWriteEditing.com.

Norma C. Mezoe has been a published writer for 32 years. Her writing has appeared in books, devotionals, take-home papers and magazines. She lives in the tiny town of Sandborn, Indiana where she is active in her church as clerk, teacher and bulletin maker. Contact her at: normacm@tds.net.

Brenda Miller was born into a Christian farm family in rural Kentucky, and married a farmer with many visions. After raising four children while working in administration for several companies in different cities, and living through some difficult circumstances, she began to write about life as a Christian wife, mother, grandmother, and caregiver. She has published two books, *God's Unfailing Love* and *Set Your House in Order . . . Reflections on God's Divine Order.* She continues to write from her family farmhouse where she is blessed with the beauty and responsibility of God's creation. Thirteen grandchildren and one great-grandchild grace the homes of her four children. She has entered a new season of life as a widow and is experiencing new challenges. Blessed with almost 50 years of marriage, she is very grateful for the love and faithfulness of her children and for God's peace that guards her heart and mind.

Stacy Mink is a devoted wife and mother who strives to inspire others through her storytelling and testimonies. She has been cultivating her writing and speaking opportunities for years through continuous personal growth and development programs and courses. She is actively involved in her church, and her children's schools, along with multiple non-profit organizations throughout her community. She is a natural health enthusiast and enjoys sharing her passion for exercise, whole foods, essential oils and chiropractic care every chance possible.

Susan Boskat Murray successfully homeschooled three children from kindergarten through high school before becoming an author and educational game developer. She currently tutors children from K-8 from her home in North Carolina.

Dr. Jayce O'Neal is the pastor of RED Church in Virginia Beach. RED Church is a growing church community focused on helping others discover REDemption through Jesus. Dr. Jayce is also the author of the best-selling *One-Minute Devotions for Boys, No Girls Allowed: Devotions for Boys, Crazy Circus World* and *100 Answers to 100 Questions Every Graduate Should Know.* He is an Instructor at Regent University and is an avid sports fan who enjoys cheering for his favorite sports teams while eating pizza with a fork. Dr. Jayce has a Doctorate, two Masters Degrees, a Bachelor of Science, and a small trophy for perfect attendance in Sunday school from when he was nine. He currently resides with his fantabulous wife and four children in the Virginia Beach area. For more information visit: redchurch.cc or DrJayce.com.

Margaret Peterson is retired which has brought freedom to enjoy time with her grandchildren. She also takes pleasure is writing stories with anticipation that they may be accepted by an editor and enjoyed by readers.

Robert W. Rettie has always been interested in writing. He keeps journals of his extensive travels and experiences. He was born in Selma, California, but his father's army career meant he grew up in various locations, including Luzon in the Philippines. After completing high school Bob enlisted in the U.S. Navy where he served in the Pacific Submarine Fleet. He attended and graduated from California Fresno State College. A position with the Army and Air Force Exchange Service allowed him to travel in the U.S. and abroad, including the Republic of South Korea. Bob now lives in Wesley Village, A Senior Living Community located in Wilmore, Kentucky, where he joined Write People. "The Treasure" is Bob's second story written for the *Moments* series. His first, "The Attack of the Killer Tamales" appeared in *Cool-inary Moments.* Bob shares his humorous writings and memoirs at the Village Open Mic Nights, likes spending time with friends and participates in numerous Village activities.

Lt. Col. Robert B. Robeson has had his articles, short stories and poems published in 130 countries and over 900 times in 330 publications including *Reader's Digest*, *Writer's Digest*, *Vietnam Combat*, *Soldier of Fortune* and *Newsday*. In addition, he has been featured in 60 anthologies. After retiring from a 27-year military career as a helicopter medical evacuation pilot on three continents and in combat in Vietnam (1969-1970), he served as a newspaper managing editor. He's been decorated eight times for valor, including two Distinguished Flying Crosses, with 26 Air Medals and a Bronze Star, among other awards. His flight crew was also recommended for the Distinguished Service Cross, the nation's second highest combat decoration. He and his wife, Phyllis, have been married 50 years and live in Lincoln, Nebraska.

Toni Armstrong Sample retired early to Greenwood, South Carolina at the end of a successful career as a Human Resource Executive, with the final fifteen years as the Owner/President of an HR consulting and training firm. Toni has written for professional journals, recreational magazines, devotionals, newspapers, and inspirational story publications. Following her husband's death in 2008 she began writing inspirational romance. Her first full-length book was released in 2014. Five additional novels were released between 2015 and 2019 along with two biographical short story books about growing up in the north and retiring in the south. Her third biographical novel, *I'll Never Be the Same*, tells her story about overcoming great times of trauma with God's help. Toni is published in various anthologies, with royalties dedicated to charitable causes. She is an ordained elder, Christian retreat leader and conference speaker, Christian education and women's Bible study leader, and commission artist concentrating on the painting of biblical scenes and characters. Her books are available on Amazon.com and other booksellers.

Nanette Thorsen Snipes, mother of four and a grandmother of eight, has contributed stories to more than sixty compilation books. She loves to spend a weekend in the mountains at a bed-and-breakfast and explore the countryside, especially waterfalls. She has authored one Arch Book for children, *Elijah Helps the Widow*, many stories and reprints in Christian magazines, stories and photos for *Georgia Magazine*, and columns for weekly newspapers. A professional editor since 2004, she specializes in children's fiction, nonfiction, and memoirs.

Rabbi Frank Stern, PhD, DD, ordained in 1965 at the Hebrew Union College in Cincinnati, Ohio, served for twenty years as Rabbi of Temple Beth Sholom in Santa Ana, California. As Executive Director of the Board of Rabbis of Greater Philadelphia, he headed an agency that provided chaplains to nursing homes, hospitals and prisons in Pennsylvania and New Jersey. Still actively involved in the Central Conference of American Rabbis, Rabbi Stern served as president of the Orange County Board of Rabbis and president of the Pacific Association of Reform Rabbis (seven western states). Until his retirement, Dr. Stern taught in the Department of Sociology and the Department of Comparative Religion at Cal State University Fullerton. He still teaches at Orange Coast College. Rabbi Stern is the author of the book *A Rabbi Looks at Jesus' Parables.* He lectures extensively throughout California. Rabbi Stern is president of the Orange County Interfaith Network (OCIN), founder of the Council of Religious Leaders of Orange County and founding president of the Orange County Jewish Genealogical Society.

Sherri Stewart loves a good suspense novel, sprinkled with romance and a strong message that challenges her faith. She spends her working hours with books — either editing others' manuscripts or writing her own. Sherri loves traveling to potential settings for future stories. Israel was her last big trip. Sherri lives in the Orlando area with her family and lazy dog,

Lily. She loves to chat with readers about their ideas. Contact her at www.stewartwriting.com.

Annmarie B. Tait resides in Conshohocken, Pennsylvania with her husband Joe Beck. Annmarie has over 100 stories published in various anthologies including the *Divine Moments* series, *Chicken Soup for the Soul, Reminisce* magazine, and the *Patchwork Path* series. She enjoys cooking and crocheting, along with singing and recording Irish and American Folk Songs. You may contact Annmarie at irishbloom@aol.com.

Myrtle Virginia Thompson (sometimes called Jenny), age 91, is a native of Portsmouth, Virginia. At age 16, she knew the Holy Spirit was waiting for her to answer the call to become a missionary. She and her husband worked in Pakistan for over 17 years. A tragic incident kept them in the US for 8 years. They then went to Iran, where she taught in Iranzamin International School, until the revolution. From there, they served a term in the United Arab Emirates, returned home and worked in the USA until her husband, who was not well, passed away. She was 85, and after having experienced the joys, trials, and blessings of a lifetime as a career-missionary, asked God if He was through with her. Apparently, not. He opened more doors. She now works with the elderly teaching Bible studies, volunteers in residential/rehab facilities and writes OpEd articles for a small local newspaper. She expects to close out her days, often learning her lessons from God's wonderful creation in the world of nature, in her tiny flower garden.

Judith Vander Wege has sold around 300 manuscripts for publication, mostly to inspirational markets including *Evangel, Live, The Lutheran, Standard, Foursquare World Advance*; devotions to *The Quiet Hour, Devotions, Light for the Word*; and many poems.

Do You Have a Story for Us?

Divine Moments is a non-paying market, but all royalties go to Samaritan's Purse, an organization that helps victims of war, poverty, natural disasters, disease, and famine with the purpose of sharing God's love through his son, Jesus Christ. Authors share with the possibility of changing someone's life, heart, or mind. Authors receive one free copy and a discount on orders.

The articles are written by both multi-published and beginning or non-published writers. Send your personal articles! The story is the important thing. The article length is anywhere from 500-2000 words or so. Yvonne has even included poems and some pieces written by children, so the guidelines aren't strict. The main point is the context of the article. (Take a look at previous Moments books that Grace Publishing has released, particularly the first one, *Divine Moments*, to see what she accepts.) She likes submissions sent as an attachment to an email, Times New Roman, 12-point type. Include on the article: name, mailing address for the one free copy, and email address. Send to Yvonne at: yvonnelehman3@gmail.com

If you have other questions, please email Yvonne.

2019 Story Callout for Yvonne Lehman's Divine Moments Book Series

Broken Moments: Times of brokenness — your own story or your observation of someone else's and how faith or a positive result helped or healed the brokenness. Can apply to hearts, lives, relationships, objects, promises, etc. (serious or humorous).

Grandma's Cookie Jar Moments: May be actual stories of Grandma's Cookie Jar. Also, the phrase is a metaphor for that warm, cozy, loving feeling of relationship. The stories might be a time of a GCJ feeling, like being in the arms of Jesus or knowing God's love surrounds us. They may be about not having a Grandma, but wanting to create that kind of experience with one's own children or even taking cookies to the sick or to a party. About a grandma or maybe a warm, cozy story having the ambience stereotypical, memorable "grandma."

Lost Moments: These can be funny stories of just being "stupid" while others may be very serious like not trusting or believing God; may be the loss of a relationship, a friend, or loved one or may be humorous stories of losing one's eyeglasses while they're sitting on your head or losing one's train of thought or someone's name (serious or humorous).

Can, Sir! Moments: Going through, surviving, caregiving, observations during the disease, cancer — your own situation or that of others.

www.ingramcontent.com/pod-product-compliance
Lightning Source LLC
Chambersburg PA
CBHW071438090426

42737CB00011B/1705
9781604950533